PERFORMANCE ASSESSMENT

Houghton
Mifflin
Harcourt

Cover and Title Page Photo Credit: ©imagewerks/Getty Images

Printed in the U.S.A.

ISBN 978-0-544-56940-9

8 9 10   0928   22 21 20 19 18 17

4500695672   B C D E F G

Approaching Performance Assessments with Confidence

By Carol Jago

In order to get good at anything, you need to practice. Whether the goal is to improve your jump shot, level up in a video game, or make the cut in band tryouts, success requires repeated practice on the court, computer, and field. The same is true of reading and writing. The only way to get good at them is by reading and writing.

Malcolm Gladwell estimates in his book *Outliers* that mastering a skill requires about 10,000 hours of dedicated practice. He argues that individuals who are outstanding in their field have one thing in common—many, many hours of working at it. Gladwell claims that success is less dependent on innate talent than it is on practice. Now I'm pretty sure that I could put in 10,000 hours at a ballet studio and still be a terrible dancer, but I agree with Gladwell that, "Practice isn't the thing you do once you're good. It's the thing you do that makes you good."

Not just any kind of practice will help you master a skill, though. Effective practice needs to focus on improvement. That is why this series of reading and writing tasks begins with a model of the kind of reading and writing you are working towards, then takes you through practice exercises, and finally invites you to perform the skills you have practiced.

Once through the cycle is only the beginning. You will want to repeat the process many times over until close reading, supporting claims with evidence, and crafting a compelling essay is something you approach with confidence. Notice that I didn't say "with ease." I wish it were otherwise, but in my experience as a teacher and as an author, writing well is never easy.

The work is worth the effort. Like a star walking out on the stage, you put your trust in the hours you've invested in practice to result in thundering applause. To our work together!

Unit 1 Argumentative Essay
Eye on Technology

STEP 1 ANALYZE THE MODEL

Should driverless cars be allowed?

Read Source Materials

STEP 2 PRACTICE THE TASK

Should people be prosecuted for online piracy?

Read Source Materials

Write an Argumentative Essay

STEP 3 PERFORM THE TASK

Should online time be limited for teens?

Read Source Materials

Unit 2 Informative Essay
Innovations

STEP 1 ANALYZE THE MODEL

Where did money come from and how has it changed over time?

Read Source Materials

STEP 2 PRACTICE THE TASK

How have ships contributed to different cultures and economies?

Read Source Materials

Write an Informative Essay

STEP 3 PERFORM THE TASK

How have different peoples created calendars to reflect time within their cultures?

Read Source Materials

Write an Informative Essay

Unit 3 Literary Analysis
Perceptions

STEP 1 ANALYZE THE MODEL

How do different people perceive love?

Read Source Materials

STEP 2 PRACTICE THE TASK

How do writers convey their perceptions of war?

Read Source Materials

STEP 3 PERFORM THE TASK

How do authors surprise and terrify readers?

Read Source Materials

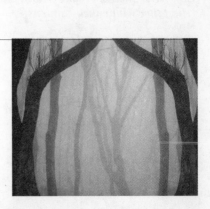

Unit 4 Mixed Practice
On Your Own

Eye on Technology

Argumentative Essay

STEP 1

ANALYZE THE MODEL

Evaluate an argumentative essay that offers reasons for and against the use of driverless cars.

STEP 2

PRACTICE THE TASK

Write an argumentative essay that takes a position on prosecuting people who commit online piracy.

STEP 3

PERFORM THE TASK

Write an argumentative essay that offers reasons for or against limiting teens' time online.

How do we relate to and interact with other people—friends, enemies, neighbors, strangers, and those with whom we may disagree? How can you speak your mind and still respect other people's opinions?

No doubt you have been involved in many arguments—squabbles with your friends, disagreements with siblings, and those times when you have tried to convince someone about something you want. These kinds of informal conversations are different from formal arguments.

IN THIS UNIT you will learn how to write an argumentative essay that is based on your close reading and analysis of several relevant sources. You will learn a step-by-step approach to stating a claim—and then organizing your essay to support your claim in a clear and logical way.

Should driverless cars be allowed?

You will read:
▶ **A RADIO INTERVIEW**
Cars of the Future

You will analyze:
▶ **A STUDENT MODEL**
Should Driverless Cars Be Allowed?

Source Material for Step 1

The radio interview on these two pages was used by Ms. Nash's student, Marion Charles, as a source for her essay, "Should Driverless Cars Be Allowed?" As you read, make notes in the side columns and underline information you find useful.

NOTES

Cars of the Future

Tuesday, April 09, 2013
by Mahdy Singh, WDRV

MS: Good evening! This is Mahdy Singh with "Cars of the Future." Last week, driverless cars became legal (for testing purposes) in California. I've got three experts here to help us understand what we might gain from this technology, and also discuss some of the risks. First, Tim Gristner, a tech tracker from GadgetGallery.com.

TG: Thanks, Mahdy. Look, driverless cars are the way of the future for several reasons. First, they are better drivers than we are! People get distracted. They text, fall asleep, drive under the influence. About 33,000 people die in car accidents in the U.S. every year, about 1.2 million across the world. Driverless cars could save tens of thousands of lives. Now, think about gains in productivity. Commuters could work in the car, check email, write reports—whatever. Last point: the number of cars on the road is expected to double in the next 50 years. Driverless cars will reduce gridlock because they can drive closer together. They can eliminate traffic jams. Who wouldn't want that?

MS: Sounds like a miracle cure! Shayna Black from *TechCitizen*, too good to be true?

SB: Well, I hate to put the brakes on your dream, Tim, but there are so many potential problems with this technology. First of all, these cars can't react to temporary road signs. They can't drive on snow. They

1. Analyze   2. Practice   3. Perform

aren't even good at backing up! A person in the car has to be ready to take over at any point. How will that work? The car is going 65 on the highway while the "operator" is watching a movie, and something comes up. How long will it take to figure out what's going on and take control? I can't picture it.

MS: Andy Green, you're a transportation attorney. Do you see legal bumps ahead?

AG: Mahdy, I see not just bumps, but, frankly, roadblocks. There are more questions than answers here. If a driverless car causes an accident, who is at fault? Can you get a speeding ticket when your foot is not on the accelerator? Can a car owner sit at home and send her car out to take the kids to soccer practice? Who's legally in charge? Who is liable if someone sues? I see lawyers benefitting from this mess more than other car owners.

MS: Tim, a last word?

TG: I think you have to have more faith—faith in scientists to perfect the technology, and faith in government and the law to figure out the details. No one thought that man would be able to fly—but now we can. While you can almost always solve a technical problem, you can never delay the future!

Discuss and Decide

You have read and analyzed a source about driverless cars. Without going any further, discuss the question: Should driverless cars be allowed?

Analyze a Student Model for Step 1

Read Marion's argumentative essay closely. The red side notes are the comments that her teacher, Ms. Nash, wrote.

Marion Charles
Ms. Nash
English 11
October 15

Should Driverless Cars Be Allowed?

Excellent hook!

Screech! Crash! The passengers get out of the car.
"Is everyone ok? What happened?"
"I don't know. I was asleep!"

What happened? Your driverless car just went off the road and knocked over a road sign, crashed through some hedges, and is now sitting in someone's front yard. You don't have to be a pessimist or a technophobe to imagine that driverless cars might lead to legal chaos.

Your precise claim is clear.

Who exactly is legally responsible when a car is driving itself and something goes wrong? Legal advisors talk of an "operator" responsible for the car, even if that person is not physically present. I think this kind of potential legal confusion arises from the fact that we are simply not yet ready for the idea of a driverless car.

Logical follow-up to your introduction. Valid reasons, well supported by sufficient evidence.

A car can be a lethal weapon, and driving a car is a big responsibility. Road hazards, computer glitches, bad weather, mechanical failure; any of these can be ingredients in a recipe for disaster. It feels reckless to give that responsibility to a machine, even a very sophisticated one. I don't think people are ready to take such a drastic step.

1. Analyze   2. Practice   3. Perform

Going driverless, we are told, will be a huge gain for society in terms of safety, productivity, and finance. A driverless car has a cooler head, a steadier hand, and better peripheral vision than any "real" driver. It doesn't do stupid things like make calls, put on makeup, or get angry at the guy who cut in too close. Better driving means fewer accidents, and fewer fatalities. Not having to drive frees people to do other, more productive work. Driverless cars can help prevent traffic jams. All of this will increase productivity and bring economic gains.

Technology soothsayers tell us that driverless cars are the way of the future. Sure, they admit that there are some technological glitches and legal puzzles yet to solve, but soon the highways will be full of people texting, watching movies, knitting, or napping as they drive to work (or rather, are driven). But not all possible technological advances are a good idea. Even for someone like me who grew up in an era when there was a new gadget or app emerging all the time, it is difficult to accept the idea of a car without a driver.

Furthermore, driverless cars will make it more attractive to commute by car, adding to energy consumption and global warming. That's the opposite of what we need. We need better public transportation, smarter urban design, and more flexibility for electronic commuting. Before these goals have been achieved, driverless cars should not be allowed.

You anticipated and addressed opposing claims that are likely to occur to your audience.

Your answer to the opposing claim is well supported with valid evidence.

Clear conclusion restates your claim. Your evidence is convincing. Excellent use of conventions of English. Good job!

Discuss and Decide

Did Marion's essay convince you that driverless cars should not be allowed? If so, which data are the most compelling?

Terminology of Argumentative Texts

Read each term and explanation. Then look back at Marion Charles's argumentative essay and find an example of each term to complete the chart.

Term	Explanation	Example from Marion's Essay
audience	The **audience** for your argument is the group of people that you want to convince. As you develop your argument, consider your audience's knowledge level and concerns.	
purpose	The **purpose** for writing an argument is to sway the audience. Your purpose should be clear, whether it is to persuade your audience to agree with your claim or to motivate your audience to take some action.	
precise claim	A **precise claim** confidently states your viewpoint. Remember that you must use reasons and evidence to support your claim, and that you must distinguish your claim from opposing claims.	
reason	A **reason** is a statement that supports your claim. (You should have more than one reason.) You will need to supply evidence for each reason you state.	
opposing claim	An **opposing claim**, or **counterclaim**, shares the point of view of people who do not agree with your claim. Opposing claims must be presented fairly with evidence.	

Should people be prosecuted for online piracy?

You will read:

▶ **AN INFO SHEET**
Illegal Downloads: Who Is Affected?

▶ **A LETTER TO THE EDITOR**
from Alma Mandelssohn

▶ **DATA ANALYSIS**
What Gets Pirated
Acceptability of Piracy

▶ **A BLOG**
A Musician's Rant

You will write:

▶ **AN ARGUMENTATIVE ESSAY**
Should people be prosecuted for online piracy?

Source Materials for Step 2

AS YOU READ Analyze the info sheet, letter to the editor, data analysis, and blog. Think about the information, including the data contained in the sources. Annotate the sources with notes that help you decide where you stand on the issue: Should people be prosecuted for online piracy?

Source 1: Info Sheet

Illegal Downloads: Who Is Affected?

Ilegal Downloads, Copyright, File Sharing & Piracy

A copyright is a form of protection granted by the laws of the United States to the creator of an original work, including literary, dramatic, musical, artistic, and certain other intellectual works. The rise of the Internet, digital media, and new technologies has prompted a new surge in the fight for copyright protection.

Digital Music and Software

Movie and music industries, with help from various internet companies, have allied themselves in the battle against illegal downloading of songs via the Internet and file sharing. Peer-to-peer networks allow users to request and receive digital transmissions of copyrighted sound recordings from other users on the network. Within seconds, an illegal file can be downloaded to the requestor's desktop.

Criminal activity on these networks isn't confined to music. These sites also allow users to search for and download pirated (illegally copied copyright material) software packages and videos.

Risks of File Sharing

When you participate in peer-to-peer networks, private data and sensitive documents on your computer become accessible to others, depending upon the settings you choose. Not all users are aware of this. The practice of using file-sharing sites also invites the threat of viruses.

The risks involved in illegally reproducing or distributing copyrighted material are significant. It is against the law both to upload and download the copyrighted works of others without express permission to do so. It is stealing, and both civil and criminal penalties are severe.

Close Read

Why has illegal downloading become a controversial issue in recent years? Cite textual evidence in your response.

_____

_____

1. Analyze   2. Practice   3. Perform

Source 2: Letter to the Editor

To the Editor:

I read your article about the case of a college student being charged $675,000 for downloading 30 songs and sharing them on the Internet. Even though I know that what he did was illegal, I think this kind of fine is crazy and wrong.

Downloading and sharing files "illegally" is very common. Most people get away scot-free while a few unlucky scapegoats get fined insane amounts that will bankrupt them for life. Some are even threatened with jail sentences.

Instead, why not fine everyone a small amount (maybe $100 a file), *every time?* The probability of being fined $100 would be a more effective deterrent than the current tiny odds (like the bad-luck lottery) of getting caught, then fined a gazillion bucks.

Remember, copying an electronic file is not the same as stealing. As Nina Paley explains in an online video, when you steal something, you have it and the rightful owner doesn't. When you copy an illegal file, both of you have it. I know that musicians and others lose out when people illegally download files, but it really isn't the same as breaking into someone's house and taking their stuff.

Let's make sure that music and other files are easily available for low prices on legitimate sites, and that when people download from bootleg sources they get fined—a small amount, but *every single time.* And let's stop persecuting and prosecuting a few people for something that might be wrong, but isn't, in the end, a terrible crime.

Yours truly,
Alma Mandelssohn

Discuss and Decide

Does Mandelssohn's solution make sense? What are other solutions? How credible is the information in her letter?

Source 3: Data Analysis

What Gets Pirated
(in millions of files per day worldwide, 2010)

music	111.1
films	11.5
television shows	2.4
computer games	1.3
software	0.8

0   20   40   60   80   100

FBI Warning

The unauthorized reproduction or distribution of this copyrighted work is illegal. Criminal copyright infringement is investigated by federal law enforcement agencies and is punishable by up to 5 years in prison and a fine of $250,000.

I | ILLEGAL DOWNLOADING
Inappropriate for All Ages

DON'T CLICK WE WILL FIND YOU

Acceptability of Piracy
(mean approval/disapproval for getting/giving music files illegally)

All surveyed:
- 43.5% disapprove
- 56.5% approve

Teens surveyed:
- 12% disapprove
- 88% approve

Discuss and Decide

1. Put into words the data shown in the graph titled "What Gets Pirated."

2. What is the implication of the data shown in the chart titled "Acceptability of Piracy"?

3. Explain the differences between the two forms of data.

1. Analyze   2. Practice   3. Perform

Source 4: Blog

A Musician's Rant

OK, listen up! Today is my day to rant against all you low-life sneaks who are downloading from bootleg sites and stealing my money!

When you download (AKA "steal") a song for free from some shady website, do you ever think about the musicians (like me) who have worked so hard to put that song together? Do you think about the days, weeks, months—maybe even years—that we have put into writing, practicing, recording, mixing, and distributing that song? Do you? Do you think about the equipment, the studio time, the electric bills, and transportation costs that we have to pay? I'm guessing the answer is no.

Hey, I am a musician, so it goes without saying that I am doing this for love, not money. It would be fabulous if I could share my music with everyone in the world for free, but—believe it or not—I have to eat! It's not like I'm charging you $20 an hour for the 10,000 hours that went into making the song. You can legally download it for a buck! Honestly, if you can't afford that, then maybe you need to ask for a raise.

What's that I hear you saying? "Everyone does it"? Really?! Last time I checked, when something is wrong, it's wrong. Period.

Look, sharing is great, and it's the source of so much inspiration and collaboration. But it has to be done in a fair way, so that creative artists have the capability of continuing to create. I want to share! Just be fair and pay me square.

Enter your email address:

Subscribe me

SEARCH

www.blogspot.com

A MUSICIAN'S RANT

Archives

October 2013
September 2013

Close Read

1. What reasons does the author give for his position on online piracy?

_____

_____

2. What does the author claim would happen if everybody pirated music?

_____

_____

Respond to Questions on Step 2 Sources

These questions will help you analyze the sources you've read. Use your notes and refer to the sources in order to answer the questions. Your answers to these questions will help you write your essay.

1 Evaluate the sources. Is the evidence from one source more credible than the evidence from another source? When you evaluate the credibility of a source, examine the expertise of the author and/or the organization responsible for the information. Record your reasons in the chart.

Source	Credible?	Reasons
Info Sheet Illegal Downloads: Who Is Affected?		
Letter to the Editor from Alma Mandelssohn		
Data Analysis What Gets Pirated Acceptability of Piracy		
Blog A Musician's Rant		

2 **Prose Constructed-Response** Do you believe that the law should be more lenient for people who commit online piracy? Explain your rationale.

_____

_____

3 **Prose Constructed-Response** If you think people should not be prosecuted, what can creators do to protect themselves?

_____

_____

_____

Types of Evidence

Every reason you offer to support the central claim of your argument must be backed up by evidence. It is useful to think ahead about evidence when you are preparing to write an argument. If the evidence is not out there to support your claim, you will need to revise your claim. The evidence you provide must be relevant, or related to your claim. It must also be sufficient. Sufficient evidence is both clear and varied.

Use this chart to help you choose different types of evidence to support your reasons.

Types of Evidence	What Does It Look Like?
Anecdotes: personal examples or stories that illustrate a point	**Blog** "... it goes without saying that I am doing this for love, not money."
Commonly accepted beliefs: ideas that most people share	**Letter to the Editor** "Downloading and sharing files 'illegally' is very common."
Examples: specific instances or illustrations of a general idea	**Letter to the Editor** "... a college student being charged $675,000 for downloading 30 songs ..."
Expert opinion: statement made by an authority on the subject	**Data Analysis** 111.1 million music files were illegally downloaded daily in 2010.
Facts: statements that can be proven true, including statistics or other numerical information	**Info Sheet** "A *copyright* is a form of protection granted by the laws of the United States to the creator of an original work..."

ASSIGNMENT

Write an argumentative essay to answer the question: Should people be prosecuted for online piracy?

Planning and Prewriting

Before you draft your essay, complete some important planning steps.

Claim ➡ Reasons ➡ Evidence

You may prefer to do your planning on a computer.

Make a Precise Claim

1. Should people be prosecuted for online piracy?

   yes ☐ no ☐

2. Review the evidence on pages 10–13. Do the sources support your position?

   yes ☐ no ☐

3. If you answered *no* to Question 2, you can either change your position or do additional research to find supporting evidence.

4. State your claim. It should be precise and explain your position on the issue.

Issue: Prosecuting people for online piracy

Your position on the issue: ______________________

Your precise claim: ______________________

State Reasons

Next, gather support for your claim. Identify several valid reasons that justify your position.

Reason 1	Reason 2	Reason 3

Find Evidence

You have identified reasons that support your claim. Summarize your reasons in the chart below. Then complete the chart by identifying evidence that supports your reasons.

Relevant Evidence: The evidence you plan to use must be *relevant* to your argument. That is, it should directly and factually support your position.

Sufficient Evidence: Additionally, your evidence must be *sufficient* to make your case. That is, you need to supply enough evidence to convince others

Short Summary of Reasons	Evidence
Reason 1	Relevant? _____ Sufficient? _____
Reason 2	Relevant? _____ Sufficient? _____
Reason 3	Relevant? _____ Sufficient? _____

Finalize Your Plan

Whether you are writing your essay at home or working in a timed situation at school, you must have a plan. You will save time and create a more organized, logical essay by planning its structure before you start writing.

Use your responses on pages 16–17, as well as your close-reading notes, to complete the graphic organizer.

▶ Try to grab your reader's attention with an interesting fact or anecdote.

▶ Identify the issue and your position.

▶ Include relevant facts, concrete details, and other evidence.

▶ State your precise claim.

▶ List the likely opposing claim and how you will counter it.

▶ Restate your claim.

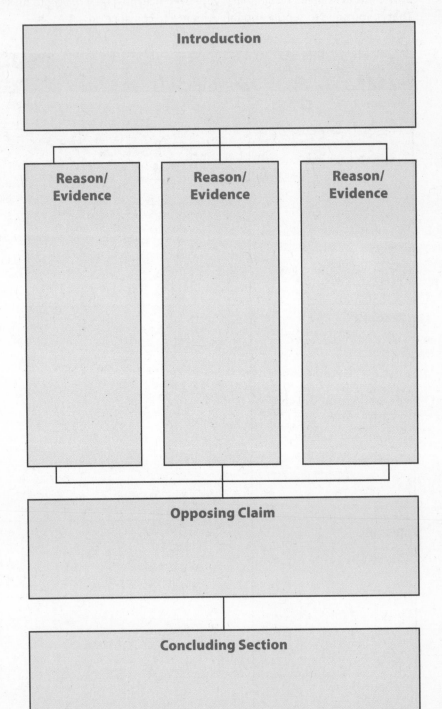

Introduction

Reason/ Evidence   **Reason/ Evidence**   **Reason/ Evidence**

Opposing Claim

Concluding Section

Draft Your Essay

As you write, think about:

▶ **Audience:** Your teacher

▶ **Purpose:** Demonstrate your understanding of the specific elements of an argumentative essay.

▶ **Style:** Use a formal and objective tone that isn't defensive.

▶ **Transitions:** Use words, such as *furthermore* or *another reason* to create cohesion, or flow.

Revise

Revision Checklist: Self Evaluation

Use the checklist below to guide your analysis.

 If you drafted your essay on the computer, you may wish to print it out so that you can evaluate it more easily.

Ask Yourself	Tips	Revision Strategies
1. Does the introduction grab the audience's attention and include a precise claim?	Draw a wavy line under the attention-grabbing text. Bracket the claim.	Add an attention grabber. Add a claim or rework the existing one to make it more precise.
2. Do at least two valid reasons support the claim? Is each reason supported by relevant and sufficient evidence?	Underline each reason. Circle each piece of evidence, and draw an arrow to the reason it supports.	Add reasons or revise existing ones to make them more valid. Add relevant evidence to ensure that your support is sufficient.
3. Do transitions create cohesion and link related parts of the argument?	Put a star next to each transition.	Add words, phrases, or clauses to connect related ideas that lack transitions.
4. Are the reasons in the order that is most persuasive?	Number the reasons in the margin, ranking them by their strength and effectiveness.	Rearrange the reasons into a more logical order, such as order of importance.
5. Are opposing claims fairly acknowledged and refuted?	Put a plus sign by any sentence that addresses an opposing claim.	Add sentences that identify and address those opposing claims.
6. Does the concluding section restate the claim?	Put a box around the restatement of your claim.	Add a sentence that restates your claim.

Revision Checklist: Peer Review

Exchange your essay with a classmate, or read it aloud to your partner. As you read and comment on your classmate's essay, focus on logic, organization, and evidence—not on whether you agree with the author's claim. Help each other identify parts of the draft that need strengthening, reworking, or a new approach.

What To Look For	Notes for My Partner
1. Does the introduction grab the audience's attention and include a precise claim?	
2. Do at least two valid reasons support the claim? Is each reason supported by relevant and sufficient evidence?	
3. Do transitions create cohesion and link related parts of the argument?	
4. Are the reasons in the order that is most persuasive?	
5. Are opposing claims fairly acknowledged and effectively refuted?	
6. Does the concluding section restate the claim?	

Edit

 Edit your essay to correct spelling, grammar, and punctuation errors.

　1. Analyze　2. Practice　3. Perform

Should online time be limited for teens?

You will read:

▶ **A MAGAZINE ARTICLE**
Teens and the Internet: How Much Is Too Much?

▶ **AN ONLINE ARTICLE**
10 Great Things Teens Learn While "Playing" Online

You will write:

▶ **AN ARGUMENTATIVE ESSAY**
Should online time be limited for teens?

Part 1: Read Sources

Source 1: Magazine Article

Teens and the Internet: How Much Is Too Much?

by Stephanie Newman, Ph.D.

AS YOU READ *Analyze the data presented in the articles. Look for evidence that supports your position on placing limits on the time teenagers spend online.*

NOTES

Most stories about adolescents and the internet underscore the very real dangers of cyberbullies, sexual predators, and on-line scams that imperil unsuspecting, vulnerable teens. Another risk? The teens themselves. Many spend hours on-line, e-mailing, instant messaging, downloading music, and updating Facebook pages, with some visiting game sites, and shopping, on-line. All of this access can be dangerous; those who abuse the internet can become trapped in a cyber riptide of sorts, pulled in further and further as their time on-line increases, their school performance declines, and their family and peer relationships
10 begin to suffer.

Who is at risk? Experts agree teens who struggle with internet overuse do not fit a single profile. Heavy users can be socially linked-in, popular adolescents who make good grades. They might spend hours chatting on-line with friends, posting photos and updates on social media sites. On the other end of the continuum are the isolated, socially anxious teens. They might be teased, bullied, and avoid school altogether. Desperate to meet people and connect, they might surf the web and visit chat rooms and game sites to the exclusion of all else.

How to determine if your teen has a problem? Take a long hard
20 look at all of his behaviors and hobbies. While all may seem well, overuse of the internet might be hidden behind deeper problems such as depression, anxiety, substance use or eating disorders, and learning or conduct problems. Experts agree that internet overuse does not occur in a vacuum. Often the problem becomes first apparent in the school setting. "Parents might first notice slippage in school performance. They eventually throw up their hands when any attempt to regulate

1. Analyze   2. Practice   3. Perform

computer use or limit access quickly devolves into defiance and angry outbursts," says Dr. Eric Teitel, a child and adolescent psychiatrist in Manhattan, and a faculty member of the NYU School of Medicine.

30   Teens might be on-line because they are already depressed, anxious, and lonely. Or they might become so, if forced to give up their habit. Signs and symptoms of withdrawal anxiety in a child include: difficulty concentrating, pacing, irritable and stressed mood, and fidgeting.

    "You might wonder whether your teen has a problem if he cannot pull himself away from the internet and transition to another activity," notes Dr. Alicia Rieger, a Westchester pediatrician.

    Other signs your child could have a problem with internet overuse? In addition to a decline in school performance and grades, signs might include repeated surfing or e-mailing during class time, difficulty
40 concentrating and falling asleep in class, hours of night-time use, frequent complaints of being tired, school lateness or absenteeism, and withdrawal from all activities such as sports practices, friends, social engagements and music lessons. Racking up bills for such things as on-line gambling or shopping is also a sign your child is spending too much time on-line.

    Experts agree, if you suspect your teen is up half the night chatting on-line, something else might be going on. "Teens who spend significant amounts of time on line can suffer from depression, anxiety, feelings of loneliness, and social isolation, and can fall victim to dangers
50 such as sexual predators," says Dr. Rieger. And cyber bullying. And we know how some of those cases have played out. So, find out more. Was your daughter cut from the team? Did your son suffer a recent break-up? Don't let a difficult situation fall through the cracks.

    While it may sound obvious, limiting computer time and access is key. If a teenager has a computer in her room or a laptop at her disposal, what she does once her parents are asleep can spell trouble. It's common sense: when you go to sleep at 10:30 in the evening, you have no idea what your teen is doing—on-line or otherwise—between the hours of 11 p.m. and 2 a.m. If this is when overuse is occurring, and if it is
60 interfering with school or socializing, time to remove the desktop or lock up the laptop.

Close Read

The author suggests that a "decline in school performance" may be a sign that a teen is overusing the internet. What earlier signs might a parent notice?

_____

10 GREAT THINGS
Teens Learn While "Playing" Online

From Christy Matte, former About.com Guide

It is normal for parents to worry that their kids are spending too much time online. Certainly, it's important that they are still maintaining in-person friendships, meeting commitments, getting exercise and exploring the physical world. On the other hand, online time isn't necessarily frivolous or wasteful. Here are 10 things your teens can learn from their time online, and some ways you can help them make connections to important life skills.

1. Typing Skills

Believe it or not, all of that multitasking online can actually help teens learn to type quickly. It's amazing what you learn when you're trying to keep up with all of your friends online.

2. Communication

Although teens are known for using "chatspeak" in their online communication, the foundation for communicating with others has little to do with the actual language used. Chatting online with others helps young people build social skills.

3. Tolerance

You can't spend time without bumping into people who differ from you due to the color of their skin, disabilities, accent or other physical attributes. As teens meet new friends on gaming websites, social networking sites and chat groups, they will learn to deal with and (hopefully) respect differences. They also learn how to cope with people who have different points of view.

4. Basic Computer Skills

Viruses, limited computer space and browser crashes are all realities of time spent online. Learning to prevent and/or cope with these issues is fundamental in becoming a savvy computer user. Most of us

1. Analyze   2. Practice   3. Perform

learn the hard way to back up data, avoid clicking on mysterious links and save often. As kids explore on the computer, they are picking up valuable information about best practices. This information will go with them as they head off for college or the workforce.

5. Self Awareness and Expression

Teens are known for exploring their identities. Decorating MySpace pages, joining affinity groups on Facebook, creating personalized
30   avatars and designing virtual rooms give teens a chance to exert control over their environment and express their personalities.

6. Global World View

The growth of the Internet has had the profound impact of making the world seem like a smaller place. In just seconds you can visit a country half way around the world, view a webcam of their wildlife, learn about their language and geography and chat with their citizens.

7. Research Skills

You can find just about anything online if you know where to look. Teens who are motivated to learn new things will be forced to learn better research skills that will stay with them for the rest of their lives.

8. Entrepreneurship
40   Creating an online business can be simple and inexpensive to do. Many teens have launched their own business ventures online in their spare time.

9. Time Management

Most teens have limited time to spend online. Whether it's one hour or five, they need to learn to prioritize their online activities. If they spend their time chatting, they may run out of time to play a game or finish up their research for a homework assignment.

10. Teaching/Mentorship Experience

One phenomenon of online communities is that there is almost always someone willing to lend a hand or answer a question. Those who are in the know are usually happy to share their knowledge with
50   others. This is can be empowering for teens who have expertise in a specific area, as they are often treated like the least knowledgeable parties at home, in school and at work.

Discuss and Decide

Which of the ten points is most likely to assist students in a future job?

Respond to Questions on Step 3 Sources

These questions will help analyze the sources you've read. Use your notes and refer
back to the sources to answer the questions. Your answers to these questions will help
you write your essay.

1 Is the evidence from one source more credible than the evidence from another source?
When you evaluate the credibility of a source, examine the expertise of the author and/
or the organization responsible for the information. Record your reasons.

Source	Credible?	Reasons
Magazine Article Teens and the Internet: How Much Is Too Much?		
Online Article 10 Great Things Teens Learn While "Playing" Online		

2 **Prose Constructed-Response** What contrasting opinions about limiting online time
for teens is raised in the first two sources? Why is this information important to address
when making an informed decision about limiting online time for teens? Cite text
evidence in your response.

_____

_____

_____

3 **Prose Constructed-Response** Does the information in Source 2 have any impact on
your opinion regarding teens and online time limits? Support your answer with details.

_____

_____

_____

Part 2: Write

ASSIGNMENT

You have read about online time limits for teens. Now write an argumentative essay explaining why you agree or disagree with the idea that there should be limits on the time teens spend online. Support your claim with details from the texts you have read.

Plan

Use the graphic organizer to help you outline the structure of your argumentative essay.

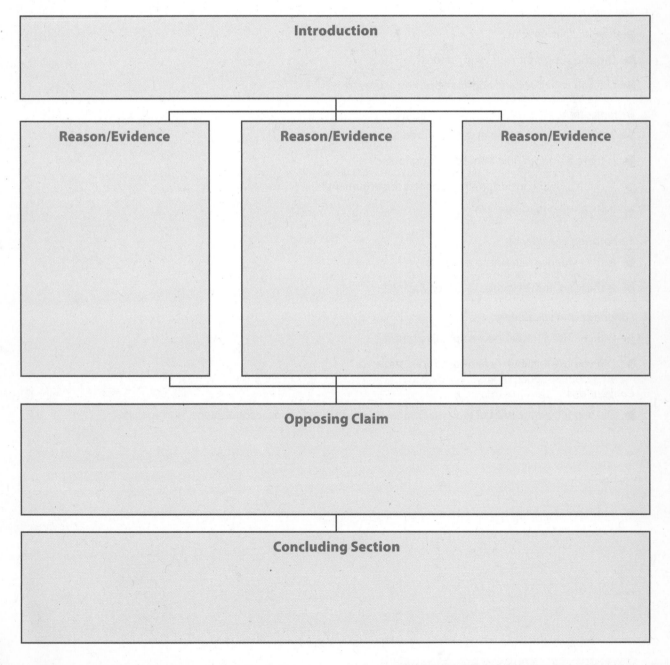

Introduction

Reason/Evidence

Reason/Evidence

Reason/Evidence

Opposing Claim

Concluding Section

Draft

 Use your notes and completed graphic organizer to write a first draft of your argumentative essay.

Revise and Edit

 Look back over your essay and compare it to the Evaluation Criteria. Revise your essay and edit it to correct spelling, grammar, and punctuation errors.

Evaluation Criteria

Your teacher will be looking for:

1. *Statement of purpose*
   ▶ Is your claim specific?
   ▶ Did you support it with valid reasons?
   ▶ Did you anticipate and address opposing claims fairly?

2. *Organization*
   ▶ Are the sections of your essay organized in a logical way?
   ▶ Is there a smooth flow from beginning to end?
   ▶ Is there a clear conclusion that supports the argument?
   ▶ Did you stay on topic?

3. *Elaboration of evidence*
   ▶ Is the evidence relevant to the topic?
   ▶ Is there enough evidence to be convincing?

4. *Language and vocabulary*
   ▶ Did you use a formal, non-combative tone?
   ▶ Did you use vocabulary familiar to your audience?

5. *Conventions*
   ▶ Did you follow the rules of grammar usage as well as punctuation, capitalization, and spelling?

Innovations

Informative Essay

STEP 1

ANALYZE THE MODEL

Analyze an informative essay about the history of money.

STEP 2

PRACTICE THE TASK

Write an informative essay about ships' contribution to cultures and economies.

STEP 3

PERFORM THE TASK

Write an informative essay about calendars from different cultures.

Informative writing, also called expository writing, informs and explains. Informative writing works with facts and can be used to evaluate the effects of a new law, to compare two movies, to analyze a piece of literature, or to examine the problem of greenhouse gases in the atmosphere. Successful informative essays examine and convey ideas and information clearly and accurately.

The nonfiction topics that you will read about in this unit describe innovations through times and across cultures, from the invention of money to the unique ways different cultures used ships and traced time.

IN THIS UNIT, you will analyze a variety of texts that convey information in different ways. You will synthesize the information from these texts as you write your essays.

Where did money come from and how has it changed over time?

You will read:

▶ **AN INSTRUCTIONAL ARTICLE**
Synthesizing Sources

You will analyze:

▶ **AN INFOGRAPHIC**
The Story of Money

▶ **A STUDENT MODEL**
The Evolution of Money

Source Materials for Step 1

Mr. Salamanca's students read the following text to help them learn strategies for writing informative essays. As you read, underline information that you find useful.

NOTES

Synthesizing Sources

When you synthesize, you compare and combine information from multiple sources. Combining information from more than one source can give you a better understanding of a subject. You can give a more in-depth response to a research question when you refer to multiple sources.

When writing an essay that requires synthesizing sources, it can be helpful to use a graphic organizer. Take notes on facts, details, examples, and statistics you discover as you research your subject. Think about how you can synthesize the information you are compiling. Then, draw conclusions based on your reading.

Source	Important Details and Ideas	Questions
The Roman Empire, history book excerpt	• Pax Romana was a time of peace and prosperity • threatened by plague, civil war, depression: The Crisis period	What caused the Pax Romana to end?
Julius Caesar, TV special	• Roman general and consul, considered a great military commander • implemented governmental reforms • assassinated by group of senators	Why was Caesar's assassination significant?

Discuss and Decide

What other sources might you refer to when researching the assassination of Julius Caesar?

▼

   1. Analyze   2. Practice   3. Perform

Organizing Your Essay

Once you have decided on your topic, the next step is organizing your essay. Putting the facts, definitions, details, and examples into a well-planned structure can help you share your ideas more effectively. Some text structures may be more appropriate for your topic than others.

- If you have multiple strong ideas to share, use a main ideas / supporting details structure. Each idea will be supported by examples and details. This structure will help you make your points in a logical way.

- If you are showing how a topic has transformed over time, use a chronological structure. This structure allows you to follow your topic's evolution in a straightforward way.

- If explaining how two things are similar or how they differ is part of your controlling idea, use a compare-and-contrast structure.

- If you are showing how one event can be the result of multiple factors, or how a single event can lead to multiple outcomes, use a cause-and-effect structure. Presenting a causal relationship will make the connection between events clear.

- Now you're ready to write. Use a graphic organizer like the one below to help you focus and manage information and ideas.

Framework for an Informative Essay

Introduction
Hook your reader's interest and clearly identify your subject. Make your topic and main idea clear.

Body
Discuss each main idea in one or more paragraphs and support each main idea with facts, examples, and quotations.

Conclusion
Bring your report to a close by tying your ideas together. Summarize or restate your main idea(s) or draw conclusions.

Analyze Models for Step 1

Read the following infographic from History.com. LeyShonda used this text as a source for her informative essay on the history of money.

THE STORY OF
MONEY

BEFORE THERE WAS MONEY
PEOPLE USED BARTERED GOODS AS PAYMENT:

ANIMAL HIDES AND TEETH

LIVESTOCK WAS THE MOST VALUABLE COMMODITY

THE WORD CATTLE comes from the Latin words "caput" and "capital," meaning property.

SHELLS

Snail shells, **CALLED COWRIE,** were so common in Chinese trade that the original character for money was based on them.

TOOLS

SALT

BEADS

CROPS

WEAPONS

TOBACCO

WEST AFRICAN TRIBES
TRADED MANILAS, bracelets and armbands made of copper and bronze

THE INCA BUILT A GREEN EMPIRE WITHOUT USING MONEY. Goods were provided by the state, and people worshipped gold and silver as part of their religion.

THE AZTECS AND MAYA USED COCOA BEANS or cotton cloths called quachtli.

THE FIRST MONEY

7TH CENTURY B.C.:
THE FIRST STANDARDIZED COINS were created in what is now western Turkey.

They were made of **ELECTRUM,** a naturally occurring amalgam of gold and silver.

IN ROME,
COINS WERE MINTED near the temple of the goddess Juno Moneta, which gave us the words "mint" and money."

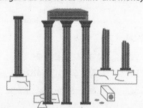

Offa, an Anglo Saxon king, **INTRODUCED THE FIRST ENGLISH COIN KNOWN AS THE PENNY** around 790 A.D.

1. Analyze   2. Practice   3. Perform

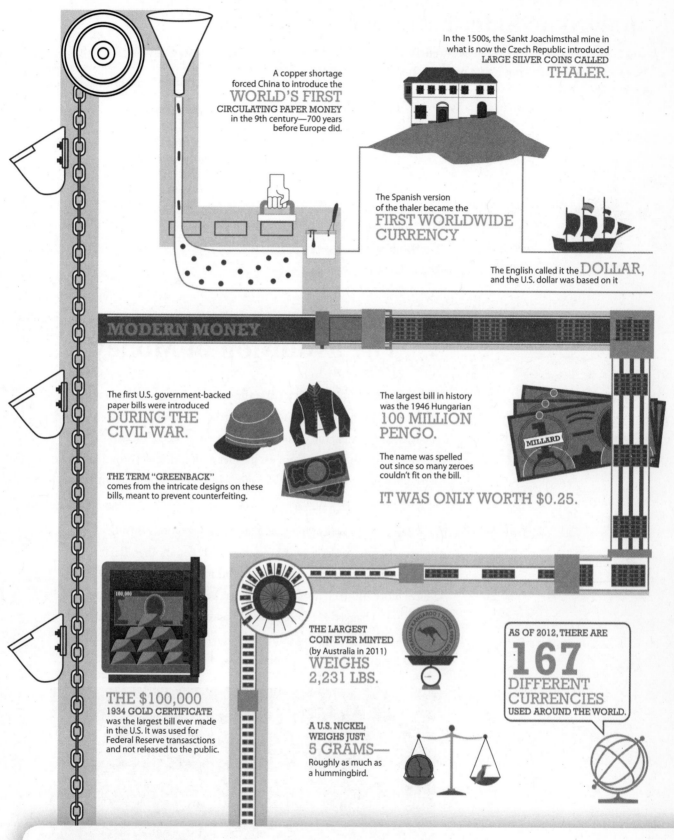

In the 1500s, the Sankt Joachimsthal mine in what is now the Czech Republic introduced LARGE SILVER COINS CALLED THALER.

A copper shortage forced China to introduce the WORLD'S FIRST CIRCULATING PAPER MONEY in the 9th century—700 years before Europe did.

The Spanish version of the thaler became the FIRST WORLDWIDE CURRENCY

The English called it the DOLLAR, and the U.S. dollar was based on it

MODERN MONEY

The first U.S. government-backed paper bills were introduced DURING THE CIVIL WAR.

THE TERM "GREENBACK" comes from the intricate designs on these bills, meant to prevent counterfeiting.

The largest bill in history was the 1946 Hungarian 100 MILLION PENGO.

The name was spelled out since so many zeroes couldn't fit on the bill.

IT WAS ONLY WORTH $0.25.

THE $100,000 1934 GOLD CERTIFICATE was the largest bill ever made in the U.S. It was used for Federal Reserve transasctions and not released to the public.

THE LARGEST COIN EVER MINTED (by Australia in 2011) WEIGHS 2,231 LBS.

A U.S. NICKEL WEIGHS JUST 5 GRAMS— Roughly as much as a hummingbird.

AS OF 2012, THERE ARE 167 DIFFERENT CURRENCIES USED AROUND THE WORLD.

Discuss and Decide

What other sources might you consult to corroborate the information presented in this infographic?

Analyze a Student Model for Step 1

Read LeyShonda's informational essay closely. The red side notes are comments made by her teacher, Mr. Salamanca.

LeyShonda's Model

Different Forms of Exchange Throughout History
Barter of Goods
Currency, including animals
Cowry shells
Coins and paper money
Credit cards
Digital payments

LeyShonda Daniel
Mr. Salamanca, English
April 10

The Evolution of Money

Nice! Likening money to an ever-evolving form of exchange is a great way to open.

The invention of money (like almost all other inventions) was a series of attempts over time to make a process easier, and then make it easier, and easier, and easier again. The issue was: How can people get the things they want from each other easily, efficiently and fairly, without theft or war? It took thousands of years to come up with the answer that we have today.

Before there was money, people exchanged goods through barter—that is, directly swapping one object for another. Barter works well in some cases but has limitations. For example, let's say I have more squirrel meat than I can eat before it will go bad, and I would like a basket. If I find a basket maker who wants squirrel meat, we make an exchange and both end up happy. But if the only basket maker around doesn't like squirrel meat, I'm out of luck.

Barter needs a "double coincidence of want" every time. Without this, an intermediary item is required—something that everyone wants or can use to get what they want. Money, in whatever form, is that intermediary object. Money allows sellers to decide if they want to spend right away on what is available or save for another day.

Nice transition to explain why money needed to evolve.

In different times and places throughout history, people have used many different things as money. The first currencies were useful in and of themselves—cows, sacks of grain, furs, or salt could be both used and traded. Cattle were used as currency as long ago as 9000 BC. But the drawbacks are pretty obvious: How do you give me change for my cow when I want to buy a banana? What if my cow gets sick and dies? What if I live in the city?

An extreme dilemma, indeed!

A better approach was to use a currency that had only a symbolic value. Cowry shells, for example, began to be used as money in China as early as 1200 BC. Cowries as cash solved many problems—they are light and small and can easily be carried from place to place; they store well, and they never get sick. Every tradable object can be assigned a value in cowries.

Of all currencies in history, cowries were used most widely across the globe and for the longest period of time. But coins and paper money are even more convenient. After paper money came plastic credit cards, and then digital forms of payment—the form of exchange we are most familiar with today. What will the future bring?

It would be interesting to see what information would be included in this essay 10 years from now!

Discuss and Decide

Do you think bartering could work today? Why or why not? Cite textual evidence in your response.

© Houghton Mifflin Harcourt Publishing Company

Terminology of Informative Essays

Read each term and explanation. Then look back and analyze the student model. Find an example from the essays to complete the chart.

Term	Explanation	Example from LeyShonda's Essay
topic	The **topic** is a word or phrase that tells what the essay is about.	
text structure	The **text structure** is the organizational pattern of an essay.	
focus	The **focus** is the controlling or overarching idea that states the main point the writer chooses to make.	
supporting evidence	The **supporting evidence** is relevant quotations and concrete details that support the focus.	
domain-specific vocabulary	**Domain-specific vocabulary** is content-specific words that are not generally used in conversation.	
text features	**Text features** are design features that help organize the text, such as headings, boldface type, italic type, bulleted or numbered lists, sidebars, and graphic aids, including charts, tables, timelines, illustrations, and photographs.	

Prose Constructed-Response

What elements are missing from LeyShonda's essay? How would you revise her essay to make it more effective?

_____

_____

_____

How have ships contributed to different cultures and economies?

You will read:

▶ **A NEWSPAPER ARTICLE**
Transporting Treasure

▶ **A HELP-WANTED ADVERTISEMENT**
Wanted: Landsmen

▶ **INVENTORIES**
Found: Ancient Greek Trading Ships

▶ **AN ANTHROPOLOGICAL ESSAY**
Canoes of the Coastal Salish

You will write:

▶ **AN INFORMATIVE ESSAY**
How have ships contributed to different cultures and economies?

Source Materials for Step 2

AS YOU READ You will be writing an essay that discusses the contribution of ships to different cultures and economies. Carefully study the sources in Step 2. Annotate by underlining and circling information that may be useful to you when you write your essay.

Source 1: Newspaper Article

TRANSPORTING TREASURE

by Arlene André

Miami, Florida—On October 31, 1755, the galleon *Notre Dame de Deliverance* set sail from Havana, Cuba. For the 500 French and Spanish crewmembers, the voyage was a disaster. On November 1, 1755, one day after its departure, the ship sank in a violent hurricane near what is now Key West, Florida. But for the group of American treasure hunters that located the *Deliverance*, the ship's ill fate could prove an astounding payday.

The *Deliverance* was part of a global trading network that connected the indigenous peoples of the New World—and the vast mineral resources of their homelands—with Europe. When sailing to the New World, galleons such as the *Deliverance* carried soldiers, weapons, colonists, and manufactured goods. On their return voyage, their hulls were laden with gold and silver extracted from New World mines, along with treasure plundered from the Inca and Aztec empires.

The *Deliverance*, claim its American discoverers, could turn out to be the richest galleon ever lost. The team provided a partial list of what they believe the *Deliverance* carried when it left Havana.

- 437 kilograms of gold bullion
- 14 kilograms of silver ore
- 24 kilograms of silver
- 15,399 gold doubloons
- more than 1 million silver pieces-of-eight
- 6 chests of gems

All told, the treasure could be worth $3 billion today. But the question of who gets to keep the wealth will be decided in court. The Spanish government argues that the *Deliverance* rightfully belongs to Spain, and France might even have a claim because the ship was a French vessel chartered by Spain.

Discuss and Decide

Should Spain and France have a claim on the *Deliverance*? Cite textual evidence in your discussion.

Source 2: Help-Wanted Advertisement

Wanted: Landsmen

Stout young men wanted for the whaleship HMS *Miss Nelly.* We sail on the seventh of December, 1794, with the outgoing tide. Apply immediately to the offices of Master Jos. Thomas Witherspoon.

Positions available:

3 Boatsteerers Able-bodied men with experience in the piloting of whale boats. Referral letters from previous whaling masters will be examined.

2 Harpooners Men who can accurately throw a harpoon from a whale boat pounding the waves in pursuit of the mighty leviathan. Harpooners must also know the science of maintaining the ship's harpoons and lances.

1 Cooper He will fashion the barrels for storing our precious prize—oil rendered from the whales' blubber. Must know all aspects of the trade, from bending of the wood to hammering of the nails.

1 Blacksmith Skilled in repairs to all manner of metal objects, from pulleys to tackles.

1 Carpenter Skilled in repairs to all manner of wooden objects, from masts to rudders.

1 Cook A strong, strong-willed man to guard the ship's rations and ensure that they last the entire voyage. He must also prepare the crew's meals.

1 surgeon Educated man with experience in the treatment of cuts, wounds, infections, scurvy, yellow fever, and other tropical maladies. Preference given to a gentleman with the stomach to perform neat amputations.

4 Crewmen Experienced whalers only.

5 Half-deck Boys Lads older than 15 need not apply. These youngsters should be prepared to scrub decks, tend ropes, fetch meals, and follow the Master's orders.

Close Read

What inferences about life on a whaling ship can you make from reading this advertisement? Cite textual evidence in your response.

_____

Source 3: Inventories

FOUND:
Ancient Greek Trading Ships

**Mazotos Shipwreck, Cyprus,
4th Century BC**

- At least 500 amphoras, some with a capacity of about 22 liters, others with a capacity of about 10 liters. Most were produced on the Aegean island of Chios

- Resin lining the inside of the Chian amphoras indicates that they contained wine, for which Chios was famous

- Two lead rods that were used to tow one of the ship's anchors

- Many olive seeds, presumably the remains of the crew's meals

**Black Sea Shipwreck, Bulgaria,
5th to 3rd Century BC**

- Twenty to 30 amphoras exposed in upper layer; unknown number below

- One amphora, with a capacity of about 22 liters, was recovered and analyzed; its size and shape indicate that it was probably manufactured in the ancient predecessor of Sinop, Turkey

- Sediment at the bottom of the amphora contained the bones of freshwater catfish, olive pits, and resin. The bones

An amphora is a large clay jar with a narrow neck, wide belly, and two handles.

had cut marks, leading researchers to believe that the amphora held preserved fish steaks. The olive pits and resin may have been left over from previous shipments.

**Alonissos Shipwreck, Greece,
4th Century BC**

- Nearly 1,000 amphoras in exposed layer; probably two more layers below

- At least half of the amphoras contained wine from the Macedonian port of Mende

- Large assortment of ceramic wine cups and bowls, a cooking pot, a bronze bucket and ladle

Discuss and Decide

What does the discovery of these amphoras tell you about the people who used them? Cite textual evidence in your discussion.

Source 4: Anthropological Essay

Canoes of the Coastal Salish

The Salish people of North America built some of the finest canoes in the world. Living on the northwest coast from present-day Oregon to British Columbia, the Salish enjoyed a landscape abundant in game and natural resources. However, travel along the rugged coast, characterized by dense forests and brush, was difficult. The ocean-going canoe solved this problem.

European explorers and missionaries in the seventeenth and eighteenth centuries marveled on the size, speed, beauty, and general sophistication of Salish canoes. A raiding party observed off the coast of Vancouver Island in 1799 included 40 canoes, each carrying about 20 warriors. War canoes were large, measuring over 60 feet long, 8 feet wide, and 7 feet tall at the bow. But the Salish built canoes for more than warfare. Trading was essential to the their economy, and many of their canoes were used to transport goods among their villages. A good freight canoe could carry up to five tons. Other canoes were fashioned specifically for speed, as races were an important part of Salish culture. Finally, of course, smaller canoes were constructed for individuals and families, who needed to travel to summer fishing villages and up coastal rivers.

For the larger canoes, Salish craftsmen selected western red cedar trees from 300 to 800 years old. The tree had to be straight, sound, and branchless along one side. More importantly, perhaps, the tree's guarding spirit needed to give its approval. Only then would the canoe-maker perform purification rituals and began the arduous task of felling the giant.

Discuss and Decide

What is one element that makes the Salish canoes special? Cite textual evidence in your response.

Respond to Questions on Step 2 Sources

The following questions will help you think about the sources you've read. Use your notes and refer to the sources as you answer the questions. Your answers will help you write your essay.

1 Which of these is *not* an accurate statement one could make after reading these selections?

   a Working on a ship requires expertise and skill.

   b. The Salish only designed canoes for river travel.

   c. Ships played a role in disseminating culture.

   d. Trading ships could carry multiple types of goods.

2 Which words best support your answer to Question 1?

   a. "A raiding party observed off the coast of Vancouver Island in 1799 included 40 canoes . . ." (Source 4)

   b. "At least half of the amphoras contained wine from the Macedonian port of Mende" (Source 3)

   c. "Able-bodied men with experience in the piloting of whale boats." (Source 2)

   d. ". . . their hulls were laden with gold and silver extracted from New World mines, along with treasure . . ." (Source 1)

3 What is different about the ship in the help-wanted advertisement from the ships in the other three selections?

   a. The ship could not carry many men.

   b. The ship was not made of wood.

   c. The ship did not transport goods.

   d. The ship had not sunk.

4 How many amphoras were there in the three ancient Greek shipwrecks?

   a. probably about 1,500 amphoras

   b. nearly 1,000 amphoras

   c. between 1,520 and 1,530 amphoras

   d. probably more than 1,520 amphoras

5 Why was it important that the Salish be versatile in their boat-making skills?

   a. They were a nomadic people.

   b. They had to carry canoes far distances for hunting.

   c. Their needs required many different kinds of canoes.

   d. They had to defend against invaders in various waters.

1. Analyze   2. Practice   3. Perform

6 Prose Constructed-Response Make a claim about each source. Support your four claims with evidence from the text.

Source	Claim
Newspaper Article Transporting Treasure	
Help-Wanted Advertisement Wanted: Landsmen	
Inventories Found: Ancient Greek Trading Ships	
Anthropological Essay Canoes of the Coastal Salish	

7 Prose Constructed-Response Choose one of the claims you listed above. Do additional research to find information that supports your claim. Then summarize your findings.

_____

_____

_____

_____

_____

_____

_____

_____

_____

_____

ASSIGNMENT

Write an informative essay to answer the following question: How have ships contributed to different cultures and economies?

Planning and Prewriting

When you write an informative essay, you need to synthesize information from more than one source.

 You may prefer to do your planning on a computer.

Analyze Sources

Look back over the sources you have read. Determine the strengths and limitations of each source by considering whether it is appropriate for your audience and purpose. Note if additional information is needed. Complete the chart to evaluate each source.

Source	Strengths and Limitations
Newspaper Article Transporting Treasure	
Help-Wanted Advertisement Wanted: Landsmen	
Inventories Found: Ancient Greek Trading Ships	
Anthropological Essay Canoes of the Coastal Salish	

Collect and Synthesize Information

Look back at your notes and look for opportunities to synthesize information—to make connections and combine facts in a way that provides a broader understanding of the subject. Complete the chart.

Topic	Evidence from Sources	Synthesis of Information
Trade		
Travel		
Hunting and Fishing		

Draft a Controlling Idea

Craft a controlling idea, or thesis statement. Your controlling idea should identify precisely what you want your audience to learn about the contribution ships have made to cultures and economies.

Controlling Idea: _____

_____

_____

_____

Finalize Your Plan

Use your responses and notes from previous pages to create a detailed plan for your essay.

▶ Hook your audience with an interesting detail, question, or quotation.

▶ Clearly state the controlling idea.

▶ Organize the information in a logical way so that each new idea builds upon previous ideas.

▶ Use metaphors, similes, and analogies to help the reader understand complex ideas.

▶ Synthesize the ideas in the information you present.

▶ Restate your controlling idea and explain the significance of your topic

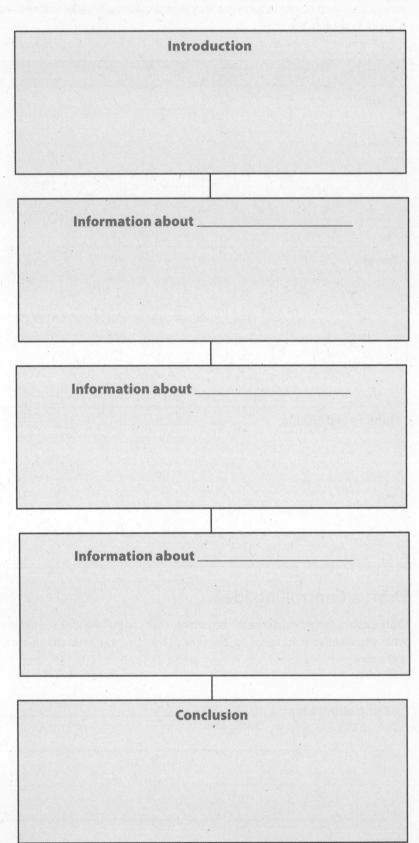

Introduction

Information about _____

Information about _____

Information about _____

Conclusion

Draft Your Essay

As you write, think about:

▶ **Audience:** Your teacher

▶ **Purpose:** Demonstrate your understanding of the specific requirements of an informative essay.

▶ **Style:** Use a formal and objective tone.

▶ **Transitions:** Use words and phrases such as *for example* or *because* to create cohesion, or flow.

Revise

Revision Checklist: Self Evaluation

Use the checklist below to guide your analysis.

 If you drafted your essay on the computer, you may wish to print it out so that you can more easily evaluate it.

Use the checklist below to guide your analysis.

Ask Yourself	Tips	Revision Strategies
1. Does the introduction present your controlling idea and grab the audience's attention?	Underline sentences in the introduction that engage readers.	Add an interesting question, fact, or observation to get the reader's attention.
2. Are your details relevant, do you present textual evidence for them, and do they support your controlling idea?	Circle textual evidence.	Add textual evidence if necessary.
3. Are appropriate and varied transitions used to clarify ideas?	Place a checkmark next to each transitional word or phrase.	Add transitional words or phrases where needed to clarify the relationships between ideas.
4. Does the concluding section restate the controlling idea and explain the topic's signficiance? Does it give the audience something to think about?	Double underline the summary of key points in the concluding section. Underline the insight offered to readers.	Add an overarching view of key details and how they support your controlling idea.

Revision Checklist: Peer Review

Exchange your essay with a classmate, or read it aloud to your partner. As you read and comment on your classmate's essay, focus on how clearly the essay describes how ships affect cultures and economies. Help each other identify parts of the drafts that need strengthening, reworking, or even a complete new approach.

What To Look For	Notes for My Partner
1. Does the introduction present your controlling idea and grab the audience's attention?	
2. Are your details relevant, do you present evidence for them, and do they support your controlling idea?	
3. Are appropriate and varied transitions used to clarify ideas?	
4. Does the concluding section restate the controlling idea and explain the topic's signficiance? Does it give the audience something to think about?	

Edit

 Edit your essay to correct spelling, grammar, and punctuation errors.

1. Analyze   2. Practice   3. Perform

How have different peoples created calendars to reflect time within their cultures?

You will read:

▶ **TWO INFORMATIONAL ARTICLES**
Ancient Calendars

How 1582 Lost Ten Days

▶ **A NEWS REPORT**
Oldest Known Mayan Calendar Debunks December 2012 Myth

You will write:

▶ **AN INFORMATIVE ESSAY**
How have different peoples created calendars to reflect time within their cultures?

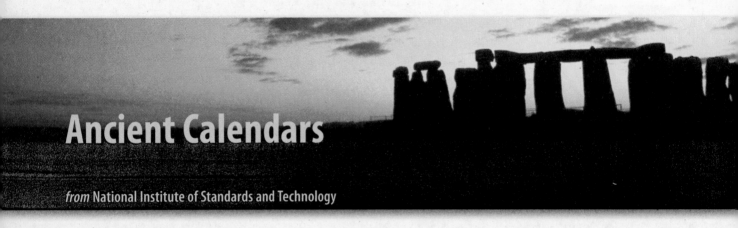

Ancient Calendars

from National Institute of Standards and Technology

AS YOU READ *Identify key terms that you might be able to use in your essay. For example, "celestial bodies" is likely to be a term used in all of the texts.*

NOTES

Celestial bodies—the Sun, Moon, planets, and stars—have provided us a reference for measuring the passage of time throughout our existence. Ancient civilizations relied upon the apparent motion of these bodies through the sky to determine seasons, months, and years.

We know little about the details of timekeeping in prehistoric eras, but wherever we turn up records and artifacts, we usually discover that in every culture, some people were preoccupied with measuring and recording the passage of time. Ice-age hunters in Europe over 20,000 years ago scratched lines and gouged holes in sticks and bones, possibly counting the days between phases of the moon. Five thousand years ago, Sumerians in the Tigris-Euphrates valley in today's Iraq had a calendar that divided the year into 30 day months, divided the day into 12 periods (each corresponding to 2 of our hours), and divided these periods into 30 parts (each like 4 of our minutes). We have no written records of Stonehenge, built over 4000 years ago in England, but its alignments show its purposes apparently included the determination of seasonal or celestial events, such as lunar eclipses, solstices and so on.

The earliest Egyptian calendar was based on the moon's cycles, but later the Egyptians realized that the "Dog Star" in Canis Major, which we call Sirius, rose next to the sun every 365 days, about when the annual inundation of the Nile began. Based on this knowledge, they devised a 365-day calendar that seems to have begun around 3100 BC, which thus seems to be one of the earliest years recorded in history.

Before 2000 BC, the Babylonians (in today's Iraq) used a year of 12 alternating 29 day and 30 day lunar months, giving a 354 day year. In contrast, the Mayans of Central America relied not only on the Sun and Moon, but also the planet Venus, to establish 260 day and 365 day calendars. This culture and its related predecessors spread across Central America between 2600 BC and AD 1500, reaching their apex 30 between AD 250 and 900. They left celestial-cycle records indicating their belief that the creation of the world occurred in 3114 BC. Their calendars later became portions of the great Aztec calendar stones. Our present civilization has adopted a 365 day solar calendar with a leap year occurring every fourth year (except century years not evenly divisible by 400).

The ancient Egyptian calendar shows the signs of the zodiac.

Discuss and Decide

How is the way the Egyptians used celestial bodies different from the way the Mayans used them? Cite textual evidence in your discussion.

How 1582 Lost Ten Days

from the *Smithsonian*

NOTES

The Gregorian calendar corrected a major error in the existing Julian calendar, which Julius Caesar introduced in 46 BC. The Julian calendar was 365 1/4 days long and the actual solar year was 365.2422 days. This meant that the Julian calendar exceeded the solar year by eleven minutes and fourteen seconds each year. This difference grew with each successive century, and by the late sixteenth century, the Julian calendar was ten full days longer than the solar calendar.

The Council of Trent (1545–1563) recognized that this growing deviation affected the liturgical calendar of the Catholic Church.

10 Religious feast days no longer conformed to the guidelines established by the Council of Nicaea, AD 325. For example, Easter, intended as a spring observance, would ultimately occur in the summer.

Pope Gregory XIII (1502-1585), elected in 1572, organized the necessary reform of the calendar. In 1577, he formed an international commission of distinguished experts to determine the necessary corrections. The commission approved a calendar worked-out by Luigi Lilius (d. 1576), a Neapolitan astronomer who had discovered that the Julian Calendar was ten days too long. In 1579, the pope ordered the construction of the first astronomical observatory at the Vatican.

20 Here the commission completed the final details of calendar reform, including a more accurate lunar almanac. These details were largely the work of the German Jesuit Christopher Clavius (1537?-1612), a noted astronomer and mathematician.

1. Analyze   2. Practice   3. Perform

Papal edict proclaimed the new Gregorian Calendar in February of 1582. This edict declared that the day after Thursday, October 4, 1582, would be Friday, October 15, thus dropping ten days and bringing the calendar in line with the solar year. The pope also approved an important reform involving leap years. Every fourth year would continue as a leap year, with an extra day in February. However, years
30 ending in two zeros would be leap years only if divisible by 400. In this manner, three days dropped every four centuries, thus avoiding major deviation from the solar year.

The Council of Trent recognized the need to reform of the Julian calendar. The changes made marked the introduction of the Gregorian calendar, still in use today.

NOTES

Close Read

Who worked on reforming the Julian calendar? Why is this significant? Cite textual evidence in your response.

_____

_____

_____

Oldest Known Mayan Calendar Debunks December 2012 Myth

by Jennie Cohen for HISTORY

NOTES

May 10, 2012

Archaeologists excavating at Xultún, a Maya site in Guatemala, have discovered a room thought to have served as a workshop for scribes and calendar priests more than 1,200 years ago. Its walls are adorned with remarkably preserved paintings and writing, including calculations related to the Mayan calendar. The scrawled numbers confirm what experts have been proclaiming for years: the Mayan calendar does not predict that the world will end on December 21, 2012.

Discovery at Xultún Battered by time and largely uncharted, the archaeological site known as Xultún sprawls over 16 square miles in
10   Guatemala's Petén rainforest. It was home to tens of thousands of people in the age of the Maya, the powerful Mesoamerican empire that reached the peak of its influence around the sixth century AD and collapsed several hundred years later. Discovered in 1915, the once-thriving metropolis features the remains of thousands of structures, including buildings up to 115 feet high. Looters have robbed the site of many of its treasures and exposed previously sheltered ruins to the destructive elements.

Oddly enough, it was a looters' trench that two years ago led to one of the most remarkable finds in the recent history of Maya archaeology.
20   In 2010, while participating in an excavation directed by Boston University professor William Saturno, an undergraduate student spied faint traces of pigment on a wall bared by looters. Saturno examined the spot, located just several feet below the surface, but didn't expect to find anything substantial. "Maya paintings are incredibly rare, not because the Maya didn't paint them often but because they rarely preserve in the tropical environment of Guatemala," he explained.

Venturing deeper into what appeared to be a surprisingly intact house, Saturno spotted additional murals more unspoiled than the first. Once he and his team decided the structure warranted a closer look, the
30   race was on to protect it from the oncoming rainy season. The National Geographic Society provided grants for the conservation work as well as further excavations in 2010 and 2011. The resulting discoveries are being reported in the June issue of *National Geographic* magazine and in the May 11 issue of the journal *Science*.

Figures on the Wall   Only 56 square feet in size, the room is decorated with murals dating back to roughly 800 AD on each of its three intact walls. The north wall features a seated king wearing an elaborate headdress with blue feathers, an attendant peeking out from behind the plumes. Painted on a recessed surface, this image could be
40   hidden behind a curtain that hung from a partially preserved bone rod. Kneeling beside the king is a man holding a stylus, possibly to identify him as a scribe, Saturno said. The meaning of an accompanying label, which roughly translates to "Younger Brother Obsidian" or "Junior Obsidian," remains unclear.

Three male figures painted in black appear on the west well, each sporting identical feathered headdresses and medallions. One of them is labeled "Older Brother Obsidian" or "Senior Obsidian," a title whose significance has yet to be understood. The east wall of the room features a figure painted in black that has badly eroded due to its proximity to
50   the exterior.

An Astronomer's Whiteboard   While the paintings are rare and intriguing, another element festooning the north and east walls proved even more astonishing to the researchers. Scrawled in red and black are charts of numbers represented by bars and dots in the typical Maya fashion. After examining the figures, experts realized they denoted time spans corresponding to cycles of the Mayan calendar. "This was a calculator, so to speak, for a calendar priest or a Maya astronomer to calculate moon ages," said David Stuart, a professor of Mesoamerican art and writing at the University of Texas at Austin, who helped
60   decipher the hieroglyphs.

Discuss and Decide

What was significant about Saturno's discovery? Cite evidence in your response.

Until now, Mayan astronomical tables have only been found in books, most famously the 1,000-year-old text known as the Dresden Codex. But the newly discovered examples, which predate the Dresden Codex by at least 200 years, appear on the walls of a dwelling, scribbled alongside artwork. For this reason, the researchers believe the room once served as a workshop for scribes, calendar priests, mathematicians, astronomers or others who would have been observing the heavens. While puzzling over a formula or predicting the next eclipse, they would have conveniently worked out their calculations right on the wall.
70   "It's kind of like having a whiteboard in your office," Stuart said.

Debunking the 2012 Myth In recent years, popular culture has latched on to theories that the Maya predicted an apocalypse on December 21, 2012. That date corresponds to the end of the Mayan calendar's current cycle, which lasts for 13 of the 144,000-day intervals known as baktuns. But scholars have long argued that, while Mayan astronomers saw each cycle's conclusion as significant, they never foresaw an apocalypse. According to the researchers who studied the Xultún house, the calculations on the walls confirm once again that the Mayan calendar stretches far beyond this December. One notation
80   in particular records an interval of 17 baktuns, a period of time that extends past the alleged doomsday.

"This sort of popular culture conception of the Maya calendar having an expiration date on it is in and of itself a fallacy," Saturno said. He compared the system to odometers that reset to zero after 99,000 miles because they can't display more than five digits. "If we're driving a car, we don't anticipate that at 100,000 miles the car will vanish from beneath us," he said. Stuart said that, rather than covering a finite period of time, "the Maya calendar is going to keep going and keep going for billions, trillions, octillions of years into the future."
90   Saturno acknowledged that the new discovery might not sway people with absolute confidence in the December 2012 prediction. "I think that as a general rule, if someone is a hardcore believer that the world is going to end in 2012, no painting is going to convince them otherwise," he said. What may do the trick, however, is waking up on December 22, he added.

Discuss and Decide

What myth do these new findings "debunk"?

Respond to Questions on Step 3 Sources

The following questions will help you think about the sources you've read. Use your notes and refer to the sources as you answer the questions. Your answers will help you write your essay.

1 Which of these is *not* an accurate claim you can make after reading these selections?

   a. People have used calendars for thousands of years.

   b. We know much about the Maya because of detailed paintings archaeologists have found.

   c. The new Gregorian calendar of 1582 was the product of religious and scientific efforts.

   d. The discovery at Xultún was momentous.

2 Which words best support your answer to Question 1?

   a. "... approved a calendar worked-out by Luigi Lilius (d. 1576), a Neapolitan astronomer ..." (Source 2, lines 16–17)

   b. "'... they rarely preserve in the tropical environment of Guatemala ...'" (Source 3, lines 25–26)

   c. "Ice-age hunters in Europe over 20,000 years ago scratched lines and gouged holes in sticks and bones ..." (Source 1, lines 8–9)

   d. "The National Geographic Society provided grants for the conservation work as well as further excavations ..." (Source 3, lines 30–32)

3 What does *liturgical* mean in "How 1582 Lost Ten Days"?

   a. ceremonial

   b. unimportant

   c. involving 365 days

   d. scientific

4 Which words from the text best help you understand the meaning of *liturgical*?

   a. "... had discovered that the Julian Calendar was ten days too long." (lines 17–18)

   b. "observatory" (line 19)

   c. "... a more accurate lunar almanac." (line 21)

   d. "feast days" (line 10)

5 **Prose Constructed-Response** How does "Ancient Calendars" differ from the other two selections? Use details from each selection in your response.

_____

_____

_____

_____

6 **Prose Constructed-Response** Why was it important to people to keep time thousands of years ago? Cite text evidence in your response.

_____

_____

_____

_____

_____

7 **Prose Constructed-Response** How is the calendar of the earliest Egyptians different from the Gregorian calendar? Cite text evidence in your response.

_____

_____

_____

_____

_____

1. Analyze   2. Practice   3. Perform

Part 2: Write

You have read information about calendars from different cultures and eras. Now you will synthesize the information from these articles to answer this question: How have different peoples created calendars to reflect time within their cultures? Include evidence from the texts.

Plan

Use the graphic organizer to help you outline the structure of your informative essay.

Introduction

Information about _____

Information about _____

Information about _____

Conclusion

Draft

 Use your notes and completed graphic organizer to write a first draft of your essay.

Revise and Edit

 Look back over your essay and compare it to the Evaluation Criteria. Revise your essay and edit it to correct spelling, grammar, and punctuation errors.

Evaluation Criteria

Your teacher will be looking for:

1. *Statement of your controlling idea*

▶ Did you maintain your controlling idea?

▶ Did you support the controlling idea with details?

2. *Organization*

▶ Are the sections of your essay organized in a logical way?

▶ Is there a smooth flow from beginning to end?

▶ Is there a clear conclusion that supports the controlling idea?

▶ Did you stay on topic?

3. *Elaboration of evidence*

▶ Is the evidence relevant to the topic?

▶ Is there enough evidence?

4. *Language and vocabulary*

▶ Did you use a formal, noncombative tone?

▶ Did you use vocabulary familiar to your audience?

5. *Conventions*

▶ Did you follow the rules of grammar usage as well as punctuation, capitalization, and spelling?

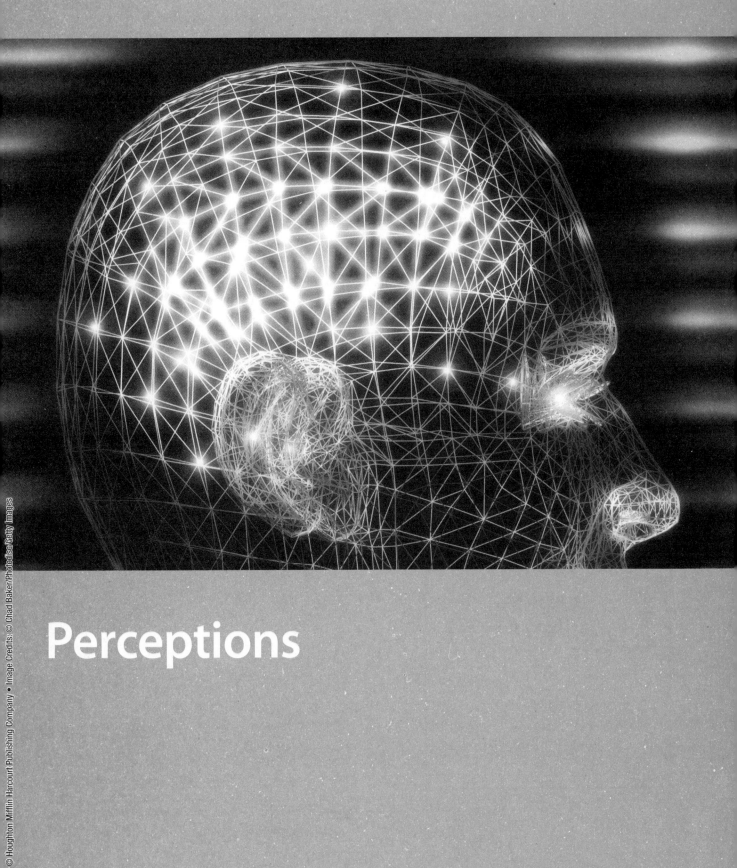

Perceptions

Literary Analysis

<table>
<tr><td>STEP
1</td><td>**ANALYZE
THE MODEL**</td></tr>
</table>

Evaluate the author's craft, choices, and theme in "Sonnet 18" by William Shakespeare and "Love is Not All" by Edna St. Vincent Millay.

<table>
<tr><td>STEP
2</td><td>**PRACTICE
THE TASK**</td></tr>
</table>

Write a literary analysis that compares and contrasts a novel excerpt and a poem.

<table>
<tr><td>STEP
3</td><td>**PERFORM
THE TASK**</td></tr>
</table>

Write an analysis of how W.F. Harvey plays with story structure and timing to create horror.

We all have a unique way of looking at things. Writers also bring a unique perspective to their work—helping readers see even the most familiar things in a new way. Authors don't just express perceptions, however. They manipulate their words to create a unique experience for their readers. The way a horror story is told, for example, creates the twists and surprises we have come to expect and love in that genre of literature.

IN THIS UNIT, you will compare and contrast "Sonnet 18" by William Shakespeare and "Love is Not All" by Edna St. Vincent Millay. You will write a literary analysis that compares and contrasts an excerpt from the novel *The Red Badge of Courage* and the poem "Camouflaging the Chimera" in terms of theme, craft, and language. Finally, you will write an analysis of how W.F. Harvey plays with text structure to create a chilling impact upon the reader in his short story "August Heat."

ANALYZE THE MODEL

How do different people perceive love?

You will read:

▶ **AN INFORMATIVE ESSAY**
William Shakespeare: The Poet and His Craft

▶ **A POEM**
"Sonnet 18"

▶ **AN INFORMATIVE ESSAY**
Edna St. Vincent Millay: The Poet and Her Craft

▶ **A POEM**
"Love is Not All (Sonnet XXX)"

You will analyze:

▶ **A STUDENT MODEL**
Love Sonnets: Comparing Shakespeare's "Sonnet 18" and Millay's "Love is Not All"

Source Materials for Step 1

Ms. Rosario assigned "Sonnet 18" by William Shakespeare and "Love is Not All (Sonnet XXX)" by Edna St. Vincent Millay and biographical essays on the two poets to her class. The notes in the side columns were written by Nikki, a student in Ms. Rosario's class.

William Shakespeare
The Poet and His Craft

by Madeline Dawson

We might say that William Shakespeare needs no introduction, but, actually, he does. Scholars are still learning and arguing about his literary works and life. Some claim his work was not written by him, that he lacked the education to write with the astonishing depth and breadth of the work attributed to him (he never went to university). We do know that his work is unparalleled in its craft, ingenuity, and genius.

> *He must have been brilliant!*

Born in April 1564 in Stratford-upon-Avon, Shakespeare was an English playwright, poet, actor, favorite dramatist of kings and queens, and arguably, the first professional writer. From about 1594, he was a key member of the Lord Chamberlain's Men, a dramatic company. His work was favored at the courts of Queen Elizabeth I and James I and was presented at the famous Globe Theater. When the plague closed English theaters, Shakespeare seemed to turn his genius from playwriting to writing sonnets (154 of them).

Shakespeare lived and wrote during the Renaissance, an extraordinary period of rebirth of art, culture, and thought that swept through Western Europe from the thirteenth through the sixteenth centuries. At that time there was a renewed interest in the classical literature of ancient Greece and Rome (Shakespeare took many stories and characters from that time), and in ideas about religion and the nature of the universe. In his plays, sonnets, and longer narrative poems, Shakespeare embodies the intellectual brilliance of the time. His work displays a deep understanding of human character, a rich classical education, and a truly wicked sense of humor.

> *I wonder why.*

> *AHA! I'm going to love his humor!*

1. Analyze   2. Practice   3. Perform

Along with the monumental histories, comedies, and tragedies that he wrote, Shakespeare is known for his unique sonnet form. A sonnet is a fourteen-line lyric poem, often written in iambic pentameter—in lines ten syllables long, with accents falling on each second syllable, as in: "Shall *I* com*pare* thee *to* a *sum*mer's *day*?" The Shakespearean sonnet, or English sonnet, is divided into four parts. The first three parts are known as quatrains, verses of four lines, rhyming ABAB, CDCD, EFEF. The last two lines is a couplet, and is rhymed GG. Shakespeare's sonnets often develop a sequence of ideas, one in each quatrain, while the couplet offers either a summary or a new insight into the poem.

I'd better pay attention to his meter and rhyme scheme to see how this works.

A wordsmith of incredible proportions, Shakespeare irrevocably changed the English language, inventing new words and phrases. Some phrases coined or popularized by Shakespeare include "all's well that ends well," "break the ice," "fancy-free," "forever and a day," "for goodness' sake," "heart of gold," "love is blind," "naked truth," "a sorry sight," and countless more. Church records show that Shakespeare was buried at Trinity Church on April 25, 1616.

I didn't know that these sayings came from Shakespeare.

Discuss and Decide

Why did Shakespeare borrow many stories and characters from classical Greek and Roman sources? What might his purpose have been?

Sonnet 18

by William Shakespeare

"summer's lease" could be the length of summer

Shall I compare thee to a summer's day?
Thou art more lovely and more temperate:
Rough winds do shake the darling buds of May,
And summer's lease hath all too short a date:
5 Sometime too hot the eye of heaven shines,
And often is his gold complexion dimmed;
And every fair from fair sometime declines,
By chance or nature's changing course untrimmed;
But thy eternal summer shall not fade,
10 Nor lose possession of that fair thou owest;
Nor shall Death brag thou wander'st in his shade,
When in eternal lines to time thou growest:
    So long as men can breathe, or eyes can see,
    So long lives this, and this gives life to thee.

why not?

Shakespeare seems to assume his work will live forever, and he assumed right! The power of the poet's love trumps time.

Close Read

In your own words, paraphrase the last two lines of the poem.

_____

_____

1. Analyze   2. Practice   3. Perform

Edna St. Vincent Millay
The Poet and Her Craft

by Steven Phillips

Writer Thomas Hardy once said that America had two great attractions: the skyscraper and the poetry of Edna St. Vincent Millay. Edna St. Vincent Millay (1892–1950) was an American poet and playwright known for her lyrical poetry (poetry that expresses personal feelings and emotion) and for her rich and emotionally complex sonnets, often on the subject of love.

Millay was born and raised in Rockland, Maine, to Cora Buzzelle Millay, a nurse, and Henry Tollman Millay, a schoolteacher. Her middle name derived from the former St. Vincent's Hospital in New York City, where a beloved uncle's life was saved. Young Edna called herself "Vincent" and was independent and outspoken—she began contributing poems to magazines while she was still a child. In 1917, the year she graduated from Vassar College, her first book of poems, *Renascence and Other Poems,* was published. After graduation, she moved to New York City's Greenwich Village, where she quickly became a part of the vibrant and modern arts scene, befriending many noted writers and artists.

Millay's 1920 collection *A Few Figs from Thistles* sparked controversy for its daring depictions of feminism. In 1919, she wrote the much-anthologized and still performed antiwar play *Aria da Capo*. In 1923, she won the Pulitzer Prize for Poetry, the third woman ever to do so.

Makes sense——love is a complex topic!

Wow! She didn't waste any time.

Millay was one of the most accomplished writers of sonnets in the twentieth century. Her poetry combined modernist literary themes, which reacted to changes in the world in the twentieth century, with traditional forms. Her poetry was matched by her dynamic and (iconoclastic) personality, which took center stage at her riveting readings. She became known both as an artist and as the embodiment of the New Woman with progressive political beliefs.

Cool word! Need to check out definition.

Both shocking and fascinating to her audiences, Millay grew in popularity even as her poetic achievements began to decline. In later life, she founded the writer's retreat and artist's colony named after her in Austerlitz, New York, which exists to support writers both past and present. One of the brightest stars of a generation was all but faded from sight when, at the age of fifty-eight, Millay died alone at her home, Steepletop, in upstate New York.

Interesting. She was already leaving the legacy she would be known for today.

Discuss and Decide

How does knowing about the poets' lives help you understand the themes in their poetry?

Love is Not All (Sonnet XXX)

by Edna St. Vincent Millay

Love is not all: it is not meat nor drink
Nor slumber nor a roof against the rain;
Nor yet a floating spar to men that sink
And rise and sink and rise and sink again;
5 Love can not fill the thickened lung with breath,
Nor clean the blood, nor set the fractured bone;
Yet many a man is making friends with death
Even as I speak, for lack of love alone.
It well may be that in a difficult hour,
10 Pinned down by pain and moaning for release,
Or nagged by want past resolution's power,
I might be driven to sell your love for peace,
Or trade the memory of this night for food.
It well may be. I do not think I would.

Life is more important than love.

Why make friends with death?

The speaker inserts herself into the poem.

Discuss and Decide

In your own words, explain the theme of "Love is Not All."

Analyze a Student Model for Step 1

Read Nikki's literary analysis closely. The red side notes are the comments that her teacher, Ms. Rosario wrote.

Nikki Yasuda
Ms. Rosario, English
March 31

Love Sonnets: Comparing Shakespeare's "Sonnet 18" and Millay's "Love is Not All"

Shakespeare's "Sonnet 18" and Edna St. Vincent Millay's "Love is Not All" are firstly alike in form—they are both "Shakespearean" sonnets, with 14 lines, similar rhyme schemes, and meter in iambic pentameter. In addition, as sonnets famously do, they both attempt to describe the mystery of love.

Shakespeare begins by comparing his love's beauty to a summer day. But a summer day's beauty is impermanent—even the most beautiful summer day has imperfections and flaws; the sun can be too hot, or clouds can mar the day. Like human beauty, it passes too swiftly and is soon forgotten ("summer's lease hath all too short a date"). But Shakespeare the artist offers a promise of immortality in the last quatrain: "Thy eternal summer shall not fade." Why? Because the beloved will be remembered forever in his poem, "So long as men can breathe, or eyes can see, / So long lives this, and this gives life to thee." Art is a kind of immortality. The beloved lives on in eternal beauty in the poem.

In "Love is Not All," Millay describes the power of love, beginning by explaining what love is not—"it is not meat nor drink," nor can it shelter or save you. Love cannot protect you from disease or relieve ill health. "Love is not all." However, Millay inserts her pivotal "Yet," contradicting this denial of love. People die, says Millay, "for lack of love alone." After painting a portrait of dire need, the speaker inserts herself directly in the sonnet, insisting she would not "trade the memory of this night." She speaks directly to her beloved now—

Nikki, great job in interpreting and presenting the meaning of the two sonnets!

Nice comparison of the language, sonnet structure, and the twists and turns of the sonneteer's ideas.

"I might be driven to sell your love for peace, / . . . I do not think I would."

Shakespeare declares boldly that he will immortalize his beloved in poetry. The feminist Millay is concerned with human wants and need in daily life; Shakespeare is more concerned with art (although "masculine" Shakespeare seems to feel every wrinkle of age pretty keenly). Yet Millay also declares that memory of love, is more powerful than enduring the most "difficult hour." Like Shakespeare's sonnet, the memory of love at its peak lives on in her poem. Thus, both poets attest to the power of love in their poetry.

Both poems are similar in their complex emotions. The poets are both keenly aware of human frailty, of the damage done by time and want. However, both sonnets argue that love transcends these things. They powerfully state how love, preserved in art, truly conquers all.

Tell me more about Shakespeare being invested in art, and Millay more in everyday life, and expand on this "masculine/feminine" idea.

I like the way you tie together the message of these emotionally rich sonnets.

Great work, Nikki!

Discuss and Decide

What other points of comparison would you add to this essay? Explain.

Terminology of Literary Analysis

Read each term and explanation. Then look back at Nikki Yasuda's literary analysis and find an example to complete the chart.

Term	Explanation	Example from Nikki's Essay
speaker	In poetry, the **speaker** is the voice that "talks" to the reader, similar to the narrator in fiction.	
theme	The **theme** is the underlying message about life or human nature that the writer wants the reader to understand.	
tone	The **tone** is the attitude the writer takes toward a subject.	
figurative language	**Figurative language** is language that communicates meanings beyond the literal meanings of words.	
style	The **style** is the particular way in which a work of literature is written—not *what* is said but *how* it is said.	
sonnet	A **sonnet** is a lyric poem of 14 lines, commonly written in iambic pentameter. The Shakespearean sonnet consists of three *quatrains*, or four-line units, and a final couplet. The Petrarchan sonnet has an 8-line stanza followed by a 6-line stanza.	

How do writers convey their perceptions of war?

You will read:

▶ **AN INFORMATIVE ESSAY**
Stephen Crane and The Red Badge of Courage

▶ **A NOVEL EXCERPT**
from The Red Badge of Courage

▶ **A POEM**
"Camouflaging the Chimera"

You will write:

▶ **A LITERARY ANALYSIS**
Compare and contrast two pieces of literature dealing with the horrors of war: an excerpt from Crane's The Red Badge of Courage *and Komunyakaa's "Camouflaging the Chimera."*

Source Materials for Step 2

AS YOU READ You will be writing an essay that compares and contrasts an excerpt from *The Red Badge of Courage* and the poem "Camouflaging the Chimera." Carefully read the article about *The Red Badge of Courage* and its author, Stephen Crane. As you read, underline and circle information that may be useful to you when you write your essay.

Source 1: Informative Essay

Stephen Crane and *The Red Badge of Courage*

Stephen Crane (1871–1900) was an American novelist, short-story writer, poet, and journalist. In his short life, he was extremely prolific (he wrote his first poem at the age of 6), leaving behind a large of body of work. He is associated with the schools of realism and naturalism, which sought to portray events and characters truthfully, without artificial conventions.

His short life was marked by scandal and adventure. He covered the Spanish-American War as a journalist, was a witness in a notorious trial of a chorus girl in New York City, and spent thirty hours adrift in a dinghy off the coast of Florida when his ship sank en route to Cuba. Beset by financial difficulties and ill health, Crane died of tuberculosis at the age of 28.

Crane won international fame for his 1895 novel *The Red Badge of Courage*, written 30 years after the American Civil War and an American classic to this day. Crane may have based the battle in the novel on the major Civil War battle of Chancellorsville, Virginia, and was inspired by reading various first-hand accounts of solders written for *Century* magazine. Despite its seemingly intimate knowledge of war and soldiers, Crane had never experienced war first-hand.

The Red Badge of Courage was innovative in a number of ways. Although it is often described as a war novel, it is more a psychological portrait of the main character's perceptions in a time of war. It relates the experience of Henry Fleming, a private in the Union army who flees from combat. The character of Henry, called "the youth" and the "tattered soldier," is an "everyman" for frightened young men everywhere as they contemplate and experience war.

In *The Red Badge of Courage*, we get Henry Fleming's impressions of what he sees and feels and hears of the war, not a description of what is actually happening. This technique, known as impressionism, had an important influence on fiction of the next several decades.

Discuss and Decide

Stephen Crane was never a soldier, but his most famous novel is about the American Civil War. Why might an author choose war as a topic? Cite textual evidence in your discussion.

Source 2: Novel Excerpt

Background: *This excerpt from* The Red Badge of Courage *describes a column of soldiers headed into battle. The "youth" is Henry Fleming, Crane's protagonist in the novel.*

from The Red Badge of Courage
by Stephen Crane

≈

Presently the calm head of a forward-going column of infantry appeared in the road. It came swiftly on. Avoiding the obstructions gave it the sinuous movement of a serpent. The men at the head butted mules with their musket stocks. They prodded teamsters indifferent to all howls. The men forced their way through parts of the dense mass by strength. The blunt head of the column pushed. The raving teamsters swore many strange oaths.

The commands to make way had the ring of a great importance in them. The men were going forward to the heart of the din. They were to confront the eager rush of the enemy. They felt the pride of their onward movement when the remainder of
10 the army seemed trying to dribble down this road. They tumbled teams about with a fine feeling that it was no matter so long as their column got to the front in time. This importance made their faces grave and stern. And the backs of the officers were very rigid.

As the youth looked at them the black weight of his woe returned to him. He felt that he was regarding a procession of chosen beings. The separation was as great to him as if they had marched with weapons of flame and banners of sunlight. He could never be like them. He could have wept in his longings.

He searched about in his mind for an adequate malediction for the indefinite cause, the thing upon which men turn the words of final blame. It—whatever it
20 was—was responsible for him, he said. There lay the fault.

The haste of the column to reach the battle seemed to the forlorn young man to be something much finer than stout fighting. Heroes, he thought, could find excuses in that long seething lane. They could retire with perfect self-respect and make excuses to the stars.

1. Analyze   2. Practice   3. Perform

He wondered what those men had eaten that they could be in such haste to force their way to grim chances of death. As he watched his envy grew until he thought that he wished to change lives with one of them. He would have liked to have used a tremendous force, he said, throw off himself and become a better. Swift pictures of himself, apart, yet in himself, came to him—a blue desperate figure leading lurid charges with one knee forward and a broken blade high—a blue, determined figure standing before a crimson and steel assault, getting calmly killed on a high place before the eyes of all. He thought of the magnificent pathos of his dead body.

These thoughts uplifted him. He felt the quiver of war desire. In his ears, he heard the ring of victory. He knew the frenzy of a rapid successful charge. The music of the trampling feet, the sharp voices, the clanking arms of the column near him made him soar on the red wings of war. For a few moments he was sublime.

Close Read

Explain what you think the author means in the sentence, "He felt the quiver of war desire" in line 33? Cite text evidence in your response.

_____

_____

Source 3: Poem

Background: *Much of the poet Yusef Komunyakaa's work is based on his experiences in the Vietnam War, where he served as an information specialist. The "chimera" in the title is a monster in Greek mythology and today refers to a fanciful creation of the imagination.*

Camouflaging the Chimera

by Yusef Komunyakaa

We tied branches to our helmets.
We painted our faces & rifles
with mud from a riverbank,

blades of grass hung from the pockets
5   of our tiger suits.° We wove
ourselves into the terrain,
content to be a hummingbird's target.

We hugged bamboo & leaned
against a breeze off the river,
10   slow-dragging with ghosts

from Saigon to Bangkok,
with women left in doorways
reaching in from America.
We aimed at dark-hearted songbirds.

15   In our way station of shadows
rock apes tried to blow our cover,
throwing stones at the sunset.
     Chameleons

crawled our spines, changing from day
to night: green to gold,
20   gold to black. But we waited
till the moon touched metal,

---

5. tiger suits: camouflage uniforms with black and green stripes

1. Analyze   2. Practice   3. Perform

till something almost broke
inside us. VC° struggled
with the hillside, like black silk

25 wrestling iron through grass.
We weren't there. The river ran
through our bones. Small animals took
        refuge
against our bodies; we held our breath,

ready to spring the **L**-shaped
30 ambush, as a world revolved
under each man's eyelid.

_____
23. VC: The Viet Cong were Communist forces that opposed the U.S. and South Vietnamese
    governments during the Vietnam War.

Close Read

Explain the significance of the title of the poem. What do you think the "chimera" in
the title symbolizes?

_____

_____

_____

_____

Respond to Questions on Step 2 Sources

These questions will help you analyze the sources you've read. Use your notes and refer to the sources in order to answer the questions. Your answers to these questions will help you write your essay.

1 Which of the following best summarizes the theme of the excerpt from *The Red Badge of Courage*?

  a. Peace is the purpose of all wars.

  b. Truth is the first casualty of war.

  c. Trusting in yourself is the essence of heroism.

  d. Soldiers are incapable of true heroism.

2 Select the three pieces of evidence from the excerpt from *The Red Badge of Courage* that best support your answer to Question 1.

  a. "Presently the calm head of a forward-going column of infantry appeared in the road." (line 1)

  b. "The men at the head butted mules with their musket stocks." (line 3)

  c. "The men were going forward to the heart of the din." (lines 7–8)

  d. "He wondered what those men had eaten that they could be in such haste to force their way to grim chances of death." (lines 25–26)

  e. As he watched his envy grew until he thought that he wished to change lives with one of them." (lines 26–27)

  f. "... a blue desperate figure leading lurid charges with one knee forward and a broken blade high—" (lines 29–30)

  g. "These thoughts uplifted him. He felt the quiver of war desire." (line 33)

  h. "He knew the frenzy of a rapid successful charge." (line 34)

3 Which statement accurately describes a contrast between the two selections?

  a. Crane's piece is bitter, but Komunyakaa's is uplifting.

  b. Crane's piece is written from one man's point of view; Komunyakaa's uses the collective voice of a group of soldiers.

  c. Crane's piece focuses on events that happened in the past; Komunyakaa's poem takes place in the present.

  d. Crane's piece emphasize s the sounds of the battle; Komunyakaa's poem emphasizes the smells of war.

4 Which of the following statements expresses a shared theme of these two selections?

  a. Peace can only be obtained through bloodshed.

  b. War requires ordinary people to perform extraordinary tasks.

  c. Soldiers are incapable of true heroism.

  d. Nature is ultimately ruined by war.

1. Analyze   2. Practice   3. Perform

5 Prose Constructed-Response In what ways are the themes of the two selections different?

_____

_____

_____

_____

_____

_____

6 Prose Constructed-Response How is the language used by the authors similar, and how is it different?

_____

_____

_____

_____

_____

_____

7 Prose Constructed-Response How do the differences in genre affect the theme (or message) in the texts?

_____

_____

_____

_____

_____

_____

Planning and Prewriting

When you compare, you tell how two things are similar. When you contrast, you tell how they are different.

 You may prefer to do your planning on the computer.

Decide on Key Points

Summarize the key points that you will include in your essay. As you make notes about each point, identify how the themes, authors' craft, language, perceptions, and other elements of the selection are alike, and how they are different.

Point	Crane	Komunyakaa
1. Characters ☐ Alike ☑ Different	Narrator focuses on one main character —a youth— although other soldiers are described.	The speaker of the poem is a "We," a group of soldiers, and does not focus on one individual.
2. Theme ☐ Alike ☐ Different		
3. Genre ☐ Alike ☐ Different		
4. Use of historical background ☐ Alike ☐ Different		
5. Events (plot/story) ☐ Alike ☐ Different		
6. Lessons learned from theme ☐ Alike ☐ Different		

1. Analyze　　2. Practice　　3. Perform

Developing Your Topic

Before you write your essay, decide how you want to organize it. For both organizational strategies, your essay will begin with an introductory paragraph and end with a concluding paragraph.

Point-by-Point Discuss the first point of comparison or contrast for the Crane selection and then the Komunyakaa poem. Then move on to the second point. If you choose this organization, you will read across the rows of this chart.

Point	Crane	Komunyakaa	
1. Characters		→	If you use this organizational structure, your essay will have a beginning paragraph comparing or contrasting the characters followed by paragraphs comparing and contrasting the other points in your chart.
2. Theme		→	
3. Genre		→	
4. Use of historical background		→	
5. Events (plot/story)		→	
6. Lessons learned from theme		→	

Subject-by-Subject Discuss all the points about the Crane excerpt before moving on to the Komunyakaa poem. If you choose this method, you will be reading across the rows of this chart.

Selection	Characters	Theme	Genre	Use of historical background	Events (plot/story)	Lessons learned from the theme
1. Crane						→
2. Komunyakaa						→

If you use this organizational structure, your essay will address all your points as they relate to the Crane excerpt, followed by one or two paragraphs addressing all your points as they relate to the Komunyakaa poem.

Finalize Your Plan

Use your responses and notes from previous pages to create a detailed plan for your essay.

▶ "Hook" your audience with an interesting detail, question, quotation, or anecdote.

▶ Identify the selections you are comparing and contrasting, and state your main idea.

Introduction

▶ Choose the text structure:
Point-by-Point Compare and contrast both selections, one point at a time; or
Subject-by-Subject Discuss all the points relating to the novel excerpt before moving on to the poem.

▶ Include relevant facts, concrete details, and other evidence. Restate your ideas.

Key Point 1

Key Point 2

Key Point 3

▶ Summarize the key points and restate your main idea.

▶ Include an insight that follows from and supports your main idea.

Conclusion

Draft Your Essay

As you write, think about:

▶ **Audience:** Your teacher

▶ **Purpose:** Demonstrate your understanding of the specific requirements of a literary analysis with a compare-and-contrast text structure.

▶ **Style:** Use a formal and objective tone.

▶ **Transitions:** Use words and phrases such as *both, and, like,* and *in the same way* to show similarities, and words and phrases such as *but, yet, unlike, however, while, although, on the other hand,* and *by contrast* to show differences.

Revise

Revision Checklist: Self Evaluation

Use the checklist below to guide your analysis.

 If you drafted your essay on the computer, you may wish to print it out so that you can more easily evaluate it.

Ask Yourself	Tips	Revision Strategies
1. Does the introduction capture the reader's attention and include a main idea?	Draw a line under the compelling introductory text. Circle the main idea.	Add a compelling introductory sentence or idea. Make your main idea clear and precise.
2. Are there examples of ways in which the selections are alike, and ways in which they are different? Are the comparisons and contrasts supported by evidence from the texts?	Underline each example. Circle the evidence from the texts and draw a line to the comparison or contrast it supports.	Add examples or revise existing ones to make them more valid. Provide evidence from the text.
3. Are appropriate and varied transitions used to compare and contrast, as well as to connect ideas?	Place a checkmark next to each transitional word or phrase. Add transitional words or phrases, where needed, to clarify the relationships between ideas.	Add words, phrases, or clauses to connect related ideas that lack transitions.
4. Is there a strong conclusion that follows from or is supported by the preceding paragraphs? Does it give the reader insight into the two texts?	Put a plus mark next to the concluding statement. Star the text in the essay that supports or builds up to the conclusion. Underline the insight that is offered to readers.	Add an overarching view of key points or a final observation about the significance of the comparison and contrast.

Revision Checklist: Peer Review

Exchange your essay with a classmate, or read it aloud to your partner. As you read and comment on your classmate's essay, focus on how the comparisons and contrasts between the themes are supported by textual evidence. Help each other identify parts of the draft that need strengthening, reworking, or a new approach.

What To Look For	Notes for My Partner
1. Does the introduction grab the audience's attention and include a clear main idea?	
2. Are there examples of ways in which the works are alike, and ways in which they are different? Are the comparisons and contrasts supported by evidence from the texts?	
3. Are appropriate and varied transitions used to connect, compare, and contrast?	
4. Is there a strong conclusion that follows from or is supported by the preceding paragraphs? Does it give the reader something to think about?	

Edit

 Edit your essay to correct spelling, grammar, and punctuation errors.

1. Analyze   2. Practice   3. Perform

PERFORM THE TASK

How do authors surprise and terrify readers?

You will read:

▶ **AN INFORMATIVE ESSAY**
How Do Horror Writers Create Suspense?

▶ **A SHORT STORY**
"August Heat"

You will write:

▶ **A LITERARY ANALYSIS**
How does W.F. Harvey create suspense in "August Heat"?

Part 1: Read Sources

Source 1: Informative Essay

How Do Horror Writers Create Suspense?

by Percy D'Aco

© Houghton Mifflin Harcourt Publishing Company • Image Credits: ©Simon Potter/Cultura/Getty Images

AS YOU READ *Circle examples of how horror writers create suspense. Record notes, comments, or questions in the side margin.*

NOTES

Horror stories are designed to make our pulses race and our skin tingle. They often revolve around mayhem and the stuff of nightmares—death, evil, the demonic, and the like. A great horror story reflects people's deepest fears.

The horror genre has its roots in folk tales and traditional stories, but it did not truly blossom until the 19th century. Some of the most well-known horror tales were written at this time: Bram Stoker's *Dracula*, Mary Shelley's *Frankenstein*, Robert Louis Stevenson's *Strange Case of Dr. Jekyll and Mr. Hyde*, and the short stories of Edgar Allan
10 Poe. These and other 19th century works have created an enduring legacy for the modern reader and are often reinterpreted and updated as plays, films, and graphic novels.

The characters in horror stories may be realistic like Hannibal Lecter or supernatural like the characters from the *Twilight Saga* series. However, all good horror stories feature a great deal of suspense. Suspense is the uncertainty or anxiety you feel about what will happen next. Writers use several methods to create suspense.

• Foreshadowing is the use of hints to suggest events later in the plot. A horror writer may use foreshadowing to suggest a
20 frightening event that awaits a main character.

- Writers may create suspense by withholding information from the reader—for instance, how a crime was committed or who committed it. One way to withhold information is to include a narrator who is not trustworthy: He or she may or may not be trying to manipulate the reader.

- Writers create suspense when a character we care about is in peril or must choose between two dangerous courses of action. We read on to find out what will happen next.

30
- A reversal is a sudden change in a character's situation from good to bad or vice versa. For example, someone is enjoying a quiet evening at home when they hear a startling noise in the basement.

The word *suspense* is related to the word *suspended*. When a story keeps us in suspense, we feel almost as if we are suspended in midair. We may even hold our breath without realizing it as we read on eagerly to find out how the story ends.

Discuss and Decide

Which method for creating suspense seems most effective? Cite text evidence in your discussion.

AUGUST HEAT

by W. F. Harvey

© Houghton Mifflin Harcourt Publishing Company • Image Credits: ©Corbis

AS YOU READ *Focus on the way the writer creates suspense. Note which methods build tension throughout the story.*

NOTES

Phenistone Road, Clapham, August 20, 190—.

I have had what I believe to be the most remarkable day in my life, and while the events are still fresh in my mind, I wish to put them down on paper as clearly as possible.

Let me say at the outset that my name is James Clarence Withencroft.

I am forty years old, in perfect health, never having known a day's illness.

By profession I am an artist, not a very successful one, but I earn
10 enough money by my black-and-white work to satisfy my necessary wants.

My only near relative, a sister, died five years ago, so that I am independent.

I breakfasted this morning at nine, and after glancing through the morning paper I lighted my pipe and proceeded to let my mind wander in the hope that I might chance upon some subject for my pencil.

The room, though door and windows were open, was oppressively hot, and I had just made up my mind that the coolest and most comfortable place in the neighborhood would be the deep end of the
20 public swimming bath, when the idea came.

I began to draw. So intent was I on my work that I left my lunch untouched, only stopping work when the clock of St. Jude's struck four.

The final result, for a hurried sketch, was, I felt sure, the best thing I had done.

1. Analyze   2. Practice   3. Perform

It showed a criminal in the dock immediately after the judge had pronounced sentence. The man was fat—enormously fat. The flesh hung in rolls about his chin; it creased his huge, stumpy neck. He was clean shaven (perhaps I should say a few days before he must have been clean shaven) and almost bald. He stood in the dock, his short, stumpy
30 fingers clasping the rail, looking straight in front of him. The feeling that his expression conveyed was not so much one of horror as of utter, absolute collapse.

There seemed nothing in the man strong enough to sustain that mountain of flesh.

I rolled up the sketch, and without quite knowing why, placed it in my pocket. Then with the rare sense of happiness which the knowledge of a good thing well done gives, I left the house.

I believe that I set out with the idea of calling upon Trenton, for I remember walking along Lytton Street and turning to the right along
40 Gilchrist Road at the bottom of the hill where the men were at work on the new tram lines.

From there onward I have only the vaguest recollections of where I went. The one thing of which I was fully conscious was the awful heat, that came up from the dusty asphalt pavement as an almost palpable wave. I longed for the thunder promised by the great banks of copper-colored cloud that hung low over the western sky.

I must have walked five or six miles, when a small boy roused me from my reverie by asking the time.

It was twenty minutes to seven.

50 When he left me I began to take stock of my bearings. I found myself standing before a gate that led into a yard bordered by a strip of thirsty earth, where there were flowers, purple stock and scarlet geranium. Above the entrance was a board with the inscription—

CHAS. ATKINSON

MONUMENTAL MASON

WORKER IN ENGLISH AND ITALIAN MARBLES

From the yard itself came a cheery whistle, the noise of hammer blows, and the cold sound of steel meeting stone.

Discuss and Decide

With a small group, discuss your impression of the narrator. Is he trustworthy? Cite text evidence in your discussion.

A sudden impulse made me enter.

60 A man was sitting with his back toward me, busy at work on a slab of curiously veined marble. He turned round as he heard my steps and stopped short.

It was the man I had been drawing, whose portrait lay in my pocket.

He sat there, huge and elephantine, the sweat pouring from his scalp, which he wiped with a red silk handkerchief. But though the face was the same, the expression was absolutely different.

He greeted me smiling, as if we were old friends, and shook my hand.

I apologized for my intrusion.

70 "Everything is hot and glary outside," I said. "This seems an oasis in the wilderness."

" I don't know about the oasis," he replied, "but it certainly is hot, as hot as hell. Take a seat, sir!"

He pointed to the end of the gravestone on which he was at work, and I sat down.

"That's a beautiful piece of stone you've got hold of," I said.

He shook his head. "In a way it is," he answered; "the surface here is as fine as anything you could wish, but there's a big flaw at the back, though I don't expect you'd ever notice it. I could never make really a
80 good job of a bit of marble like that. It would be all right in the summer like this; it wouldn't mind the blasted heat. But wait till the winter comes. There's nothing like frost to find out the weak points in stone."

"Then what's it for?" I asked.

The man burst out laughing.

"You'd hardly believe me if I was to tell you it's for an exhibition, but it's the truth. Artists have exhibitions; so do grocers and butchers; we have them too. All the latest little things in headstones, you know."

He went on to talk of marbles, which sort best withstood wind and rain, and which were easiest to work; then of his garden and a new sort
90 of carnation he had bought. At the end of every other minute he would drop his tools, wipe his shining head, and curse the heat.

I said little, for I felt uneasy. There was something unnatural, uncanny, in meeting this man.

I tried at first to persuade myself that I had seen him before, that his face, unknown to me, had found a place in some out-of-the-way corner of my memory, but I knew that I was practicing little more than a plausible piece of self-deception.

Mr. Atkinson finished his work, spat on the ground, and got up with a sigh of relief.

100 "There! What do you think of that?" he said, with an air of evident pride.

The inscription which I read for the first time was this—

SACRED TO THE MEMORY

OF

JAMES CLARENCE WITHENCROFT

BORN JAN. 18TH, 1860

HE PASSED AWAY VERY SUDDENLY

ON AUGUST 20TH, 190—

"In the midst of life we are in death."

110 For some time I sat in silence. Then a cold shudder ran down my spine. I asked him where he had seen the name.

"Oh, I didn't see it anywhere," replied Mr. Atkinson. "I wanted some name, and I put down the first that came into my head. Why do you want to know?"

"It's a strange coincidence, but it happens to be mine."

He gave a long, low whistle.

"And the dates?"

"I can only answer for one of them, and that's correct."

"It's a rum go!" he said.

120 But he knew less than I did. I told him of my morning's work. I took the sketch from my pocket and showed it to him. As he looked, the expression of his face altered until it became more and more like that of the man I had drawn.

"And it was only the day before yesterday," he said, "that I told Maria there were no such things as ghosts!"

Neither of us had seen a ghost, but I knew what he meant.

"You probably heard my name," I said.

"And you must have seen me somewhere and have forgotten it!

Discuss and Decide

With a small group, list three details that create suspense. Cite specific text evidence to justify your choices.

Were you at Clacton-on-Sea last July?"

130   I had never been to Clacton in my life. We were silent for some
time. We were both looking at the same thing, the two dates on the
gravestone, and one was right.

"Come inside and have some supper," said Mr. Atkinson.

His wife was a cheerful little woman, with the flaky red cheeks of
the country-bred. Her husband introduced me as a friend of his who
was an artist. The result was unfortunate, for after the sardines and
watercress had been removed, she brought me out a Doré Bible, and I
had to sit and express my admiration for nearly half an hour.

I went outside, and found Atkinson sitting on the gravestone

140   smoking.

We resumed the conversation at the point we had left off.

"You must excuse my asking," I said, "but do you know of anything
you've done for which you could be put on trial?"

He shook his head.

"I'm not a bankrupt, the business is prosperous enough. Three
years ago I gave turkeys to some of the guardians at Christmas, but
that's all I can think of. And they were small ones, too," he added as an
afterthought.

He got up, fetched a can from the porch, and began to water the

150   flowers. "Twice a day regular in the hot weather," he said, "and then
the heat sometimes gets the better of the delicate ones. And ferns, good
Lord! They could never stand it. Where do you live?"

I told him my address. It would take an hour's quick walk to get back home.

"It's like this,' he said. "We'll look at the matter straight. If you go back home to-night, you take your chance of accidents. A cart may run over you, and there's always banana skins and orange peel, to say nothing of fallen ladders."

He spoke of the improbable with an intense seriousness that would
160 have been laughable six hours before. But l did not laugh.

"The best thing we can do," he continued, "is for you to stay here till twelve o'clock. We'll go upstairs and smoke; it may be cooler inside.'

To my surprise, I agreed.

We are sitting in a long, low room beneath the eaves. Atkinson has sent his wife to bed. He himself is busy sharpening some tools at a little oilstone, smoking one of my cigars the while.

The air seemed charged with thunder. I am writing this at a shaky table before the open window. The leg is cracked, and Atkinson, who seems a handy man with his tools, is going to mend it as soon as he has
170 finished putting an edge on his chisel.

It is after eleven now. I shall be gone in less than an hour.

But the heat is stifling.

It is enough to send a man mad.

Close Read

What do you think is going to happen to the narrator? Cite text evidence in your response.

_____

_____

_____

_____

Respond to Questions on Step 3 Sources

These questions will help you think about the informational essay and the short story that you have read. Use your notes and refer to the sources in order to answer the questions. Your answers to these questions will help you write your essay.

1 **Prose Constructed-Response** What is mysterious about the events in lines 50–63? Cite specific evidence from the text.

_____

_____

_____

_____

_____

2 **Prose Constructed-Response** What events in the story does the author foreshadow? What clues hint at these events? Cite text evidence in your response.

_____

_____

_____

_____

_____

3 **Prose Constructed-Response** How does the ending create a frightening effect? Cite text evidence in your response.

_____

_____

_____

_____

_____

_____

Part 2: Write

Plan

Use the graphic organizer to help you outline the structure of your literary analysis.

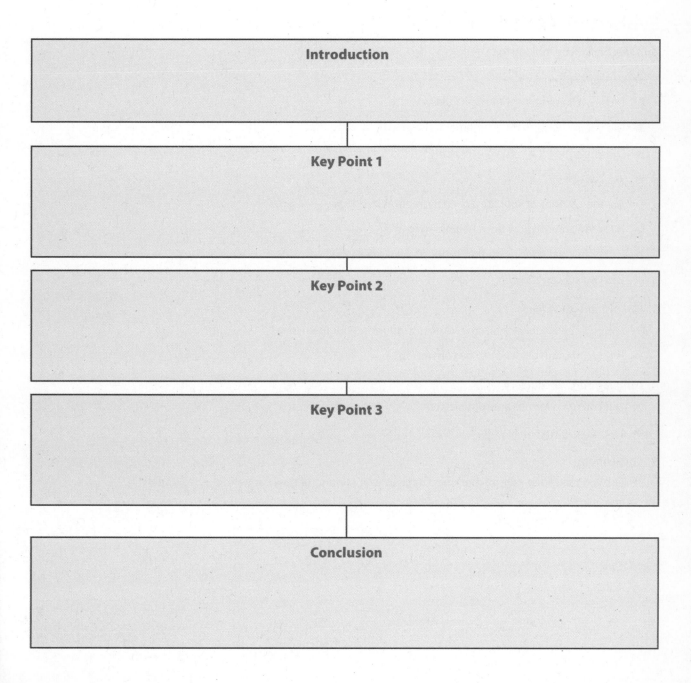

Introduction

Key Point 1

Key Point 2

Key Point 3

Conclusion

Draft

 Use your notes and completed graphic organizer to write a first draft of your literary analysis.

Revise and Edit

 Look back over your essay and compare it to the Evaluation Criteria. Revise your literary analysis and edit it to correct spelling, grammar, and punctuation errors.

Evaluation Criteria

Your teacher will be looking for:

1. *Statement of purpose*
   ▶ Did you clearly state your main idea?
   ▶ Did you respond to the assignment question?
   ▶ Did you support it with valid reasons?

2. *Organization*
   ▶ Are the sections of your literary analysis organized in a logical way?
   ▶ Is there a smooth flow from beginning to end?
   ▶ Is there a clear conclusion that supports your main idea?
   ▶ Did you stay on topic?

3. *Elaboration of evidence*
   ▶ Did you cite evidence from the sources to support your main idea?
   ▶ Is there enough evidence to be convincing?

4. *Language and vocabulary*
   ▶ Did you use a formal, appropriate tone?
   ▶ Did you use vocabulary familiar to your audience?

5. *Conventions*
   ▶ Did you follow the rules of grammar usage as well as punctuation, capitalization, and spelling?

On Your Own

TASK 1

Argumentative Essay

Your local school board is debating a policy that includes mandatory community service for high school graduation. You have been asked to write an argumentative essay on the topic that will be presented at the next school board meeting.

First you will review two sources about community service requirements for students. After you have reviewed these sources, you will answer some questions about them. You should first skim the sources and the questions and then go back and read them carefully.

In Part 2, you will write an argumentative essay about whether you agree or disagree that community service should be a requirement for high school graduation.

Time Management: Argumentative Task

There are two parts to most formal writing tests. Both parts of the tests are timed, so it's important to use your limited time wisely.

Part 1: Read Sources and Answer Questions

Preview the Assignment

35 minutes

35 minutes! That's not much time.

You will have 35 minutes to read two articles about the pros and cons of mandatory community service for students. You will also answer questions about the sources that will help you plan your essay.

How Many?

Preview the questions so you'll know which information you'll need to find as you read.

How many pages of reading?

→ How many multiple-choice questions?

→ How many prose constructed-response questions?

How do you plan to use the 35 minutes?

Underline, circle, and take notes as you read. You probably won't have time to reread.

Estimated time to read:

This is a lot to do in a short time.

Source #1: "Volunteering to Graduate..."   _____ minutes

Source #2: "Pro/Con: Should student service learning hours be mandatory . . . ?"   _____ minutes

Estimated time to answer questions?   _____ minutes

Total   **35   minutes**

Any concerns?

_____

_____

_____

_____

Part 2: Write the Essay

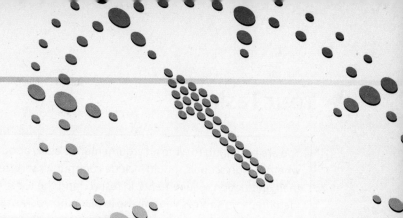

How much time do you have? Pay attention to the clock!

Plan and Write an Argumentative Essay

85 minutes

You will have 85 minutes to plan, write, revise, and edit your essay.

Your Plan

Before you start to write, decide on your precise claim. Then think about the evidence you will use to support your claim.

How do you plan to use the 85 minutes?

Be sure to leave enough time for this step.

Estimated time for planning the essay?		minutes
Estimated time for writing?		minutes
Estimated time for editing?		minutes
Estimated time for checking spelling, grammar, and punctuation?		minutes
Total	**85**	**minutes**

Notes:

_____

_____

_____

_____

Reread your essay, making sure that the points are clear. Check that there are no spelling or punctuation mistakes.

▶ Your Task

You are preparing to write an argumentative essay about whether high schools should include community service among their graduation requirements. In researching the topic, you have identified two sources you will use in planning your essay.

After you have reviewed the sources, you must answer some questions about them. Briefly skim the sources and the questions that follow. Then, go back and read the sources carefully so you will have the information you will need to answer the questions. Take notes on the sources as you read. You may refer back to your notes at any time during Part 1 or Part 2 of the performance task.

▶ Part 1 (35 minutes)

You will now read the sources. After carefully reading the sources, use the rest of the time in Part 1 to answer the three questions about them. Though your answers to these questions will help you think about what you have read and plan your essay, they will also be scored as part of the test.

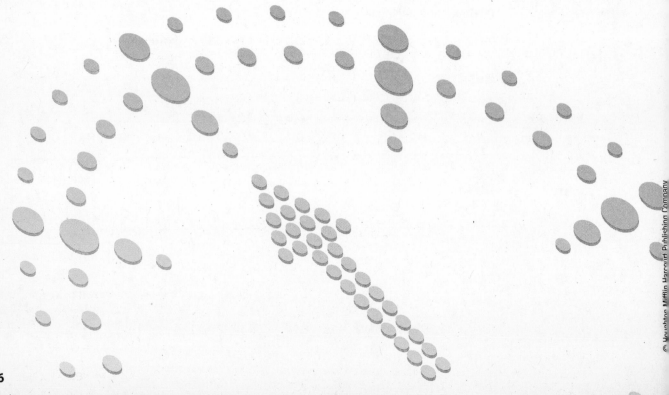

SOURCE #1:
Volunteering to Graduate: Do We Need More Requirements?

by Miriam Dodge

The following editorial about adding community service to graduation requirements was written by one student for her school newspaper.

NOTES

The query posed in the title above may sound like a rhetorical question, but the issue of required volunteer hours for high school students has become a much-debated topic. A number of American high schools have made the completion of a certain number of community service hours a requirement for graduating.

Those who support the requirement do so with good reason. Participating in volunteer work can help students in many ways. It requires them to schedule their time and learn how to juggle responsibilities. The ability to multitask is a skill that they will need
10 in both work and college environments. Students learn the value of responsibility and discipline, as well as the value of giving back to their community. Students who participate in community service tend to graduate at a higher rate than students who do not engage in such activity.

Not all students—or parents—support this mandate as an additional criterion to required coursework. For one thing, making a selfless act a requirement for graduating negates the spirit of volunteerism itself. If a student gives only to get in return, that does not teach him or her the true value of donating time. The student will not
20 feel the reward of having spent time charitably, and may not be inclined to volunteer in the future. Having an added requirement for graduating turns an already stressful year, a year full of college applications, final exams, GPA tallies, after-school jobs, extracurricular activities, and goodbyes to classmates into a mad rush of meeting deadlines. Finally, enforced community service is a form of penance for those who have committed a punishable crime—should the same service be asked of high school students?

Am I on Track?

Actual Time Spent Reading

SOURCE #2:

Pro/Con: Should student service learning hours be mandatory for high school graduation?

by Claire Koenig, Print Managing Op/Ed Editor and
Simrin Gupta, Print Managing Entertainment Editor, *Silver Chips Online*   *March 10, 2011*

NOTES

Simrin Gupta says yes: The SSL hour requirement benefits the community and encourages responsibility.

Picking up trash might not be the average teenager's idea of a fun weekend activity. But as students complete their Student Service Learning (SSL) hour requirement cleaning up the environment, they end up picking up a lot more than trash. For years, high school students have been giving back to the community through the SSL hour requirement. As a result, causes across the community have benefitted and students have taken on a new sense of responsibility. The SSL hour

10   requirement lets students establish social partnerships while addressing recognized needs.

The purpose of SSL hours is to address community needs in a way that reinforces curriculum goals because they arm students with the knowledge, skills and attitude necessary for productivity in an increasingly diverse and interconnected world. According to the original 1997 MCPS memo, all community service action, whether it be direct or indirect, encourages career preparation and reflection.

First and foremost, the SSL hour requirement teaches students responsibility. Regardless of the type of activity they decide to pursue,

20   students are held responsible for completing a job to the best of their ability. This sense of accountability contributes to an overarching feeling of personal responsibility. Furthermore, according to Blair Student Service Learning Coordinator Robert Hopkins, "The greatest part of SSL hours is that students learn transferable skills that can be applied to a variety of unique situations," he says.

More importantly, the SSL hour requirement prompts experiences that can form links to what students learn at school. These learning links reinforce the concepts students have been introduced to at school. Throughout elementary, middle and high school, MCPS [Montgomery

30   County Public Schools] students learn about major issues like natural disasters and ecosystem conservation, as well as societal issues like bullying prevention, nutrition and fitness. For example, a student with a particular interest in environmental science puts their knowledge to

the test when they volunteer with organizations like the Seneca Creek State Park or the C&O Canal Association. Even when activism is not directly related to coursework, students learn universal lessons like the importance of helping their fellow community members when they help feed the homeless or build homes for natural disaster victims. By fulfilling this requirement, students also gain the opportunity to

40   volunteer in fields that interest them, allowing them to experiment with possible career paths.

But perhaps the most beneficial part of the SSL hour requirement is that it gives students experience with group dynamics. When performing community service, students learn to form a cooperative team in order to accomplish their goal. They have to effectively work with members in authority positions as well. When they dedicate time to the community, students make attitudinal and behavioral strides by learning how to be productive members of society. According to Julie Ayers, a service-learning specialist for the Maryland State Department

50   of Education, the hours students spend doing community service equip them with the knowledge and skills needed for civic engagement.

Instead of taking a more lax approach regarding the SSL hour requirement, MCPS should continue to make the hours mandatory for graduation. Though a 15-hour increase may strike some as a burden, it's 15 more hours during which students are learning skills crucial to their future success. Without the consequence of not graduating, the majority of students may not be exposed to the numerous advantages of community service work. The community benefits from students' work, and students take away experiences that enable them to live successfully.

60   **Claire Koenig says no: Mandated community service takes away from the meaning of the experience.**

What happened to asking what we can do for our country? All for one and one for all? It's a small world? Apparently, the school system feels that there isn't enough kumbaya to go around, so it has chosen to make service a part of the graduation requirement.

The Student Service Learning (SSL) obligation imposed upon high school students today is not only unfair, but unnecessary. The initiative to serve the community shouldn't have to come from fear of failing to graduate, but from a student's passions and interests.

70   The obvious merit of community service is not debatable—students learn to appreciate lending a hand while non-profits put those hands to good use. But the logic of forcing people to volunteer falls short when compared to the benefits students gain from the act of offering

to perform community service. Schools should do all they can to encourage students to volunteer by continuing to provide opportunities in the community and rewarding students who complete an exemplary number of hours, but community service should not be required in order to achieve a high school diploma.

The merit of volunteer work stems from the fact that it is voluntary —if schools mandate that students perform community service, then projects lose value to the student participants. Many students don't feel inspired by their time serving the community so much as irritated that they were forced to do so by the school system in the same way that some children disregard good advice because it comes from their parents.

The SSL requirement can also be insulting to those that are enthusiastic about their volunteer work. These students should be proud that they can help selflessly out of intrinsic motivation, instead of feeling forced to put their hours of hard work towards an SSL requirement. The 1992 district court case Steirer v. Bethlehem Area School District highlighted this dilemma when two students dedicated to their service work appealed to the court for their diplomas after refusing to put their volunteer hours toward the community service requirement. Although the court's verdict came back against the students' plea, the message they sought to send is clear: They performed community service for good, not for graduation.

High school is a busy time—many students juggle jobs or multiple afterschool activities in addition to their schoolwork. It is unfair to those students who have obligations outside of school to keep them from graduating because of SSL hours, because some of them simply don't have the time to spare.

In some cases service hours are the barrier keeping students from graduating. Encouraging good work for a good cause is one thing; driving students to the good work for the sake of graduating is another.

While it is true that the required hours of service do open students to work in the community that they would not experience should the mandate be eliminated, but the SSL requirement also enforces the wrong mindset toward community service in students.

As it is, MCPS is encouraging students to do the right things for all the wrong reasons.

Am I on Track?

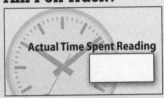

Actual Time Spent Reading

Part 1 Questions

Answer the following questions. Your answers to these questions will be scored. You may refer to your reading notes, and you should cite text evidence in your responses. You will be able to refer to your answers as you write your essay in Part 2.

1 Using context clues, choose the **best** synonym for the word *exemplary* as it is used in the following sentence from Source #2: "Schools should do all they can to encourage students to volunteer by continuing to provide opportunities in the community and rewarding students who complete an exemplary number of hours, but community service should not be required in order to achieve a high school diploma."

   a. deplorable

   b. commendable

   c. temporary

   d. exhausting

2 **Prose Constructed-Response** Write a brief summary of Source #1 in the lines below. Use your own words, and make sure your summary is free from bias or opinion.

_____

_____

_____

_____

_____

_____

3 **Prose Constructed-Response** In Source #2, what does Simrin Gupta say is the most beneficial aspect of mandatory community service? What does Claire Koenig suggest as an alternative to mandatory community service? Support your response with evidence from the source.

_____

_____

_____

_____

_____

_____

▶ Part 2 (85 minutes)

You will have 85 minutes to review your notes and sources, and to plan, draft, edit, and revise your essay. While you may use your notes and refer to the sources, your essay must represent your original work. You may refer to your responses to Part 1, but you cannot change those answers. Now read your assignment and the information about how your writing will be scored; then begin your work.

Your Assignment

It is time to begin writing your argumentative essay for the school board meeting. Remember, your essay should explain whether you agree or disagree that high school students should be required to do community service in order to graduate. When writing your essay, find ways to use information from the two sources to support your argument. A good argumentative essay should include a strong claim, and it should address opposing arguments.

Argumentative Essay Scoring

Your essay will be scored using the following:

1. **Organization/purpose:** How well did you express your claim, address opposing claims, and support your claim with logical ideas? How well did your ideas flow from beginning to end? How effective was your introduction and conclusion?

2. **Evidence/elaboration:** How well did you incorporate relevant information from the sources? Did you use specific titles or numbers in referring to the sources? How strong is the elaboration for your ideas? Did you clearly state your ideas in your own words in a way that is appropriate for your audience and purpose?

3. **Conventions:** How well did you follow the rules of grammar, punctuation, capitalization, and spelling?

Now begin work on your essay. Manage your time carefully so that you can:

- plan your essay, using your notes

- write your essay

- revise and edit your final draft

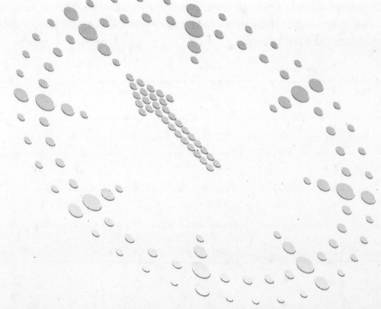

TASK 2

RESEARCH SIMULATION

Informative Essay

Your health teacher has asked the students in your class to write an informative essay about outdoor recreation. You have been assigned the topic of geocaching.

First you will review two articles about issues surrounding geocaching. After you have reviewed these sources, you will answer some questions about them. You should first skim the sources and the questions and then go back and read them carefully.

In Part 2, you will write an informative essay about geocaching and the controversy surrounding it.

Time Management: Informative Task

There are two parts to most formal writing tests. Both parts of the tests are timed, so it's important to use your limited time wisely.

Part 1: Read Sources and Answer Questions

Preview the Assignment

35 minutes

You will have 35 minutes to read two sources about geocaching. You will also answer questions about these two sources.

35 minutes! That's not much time.

How Many?

Preview the questions so you'll know which information you'll need to find as you read.

How many pages of reading?

→ How many multiple-choice questions?

→ How many prose constructed-response questions?

How do you plan to use the 35 minutes?

Underline, circle, and take notes as you read. You probably won't have time to reread.

This is a lot to do in a short time.

Estimated time to read:

    Source #1: "Geocaching" — _____ minutes

    Source #2: "Seattle Firm's GPS Scavenger-Hunt Game Stirs Controversy" — _____ minutes

Estimated time to answer questions? — _____ minutes

Total   **35**   **minutes**

Any concerns?

_____

_____

_____

_____

Part 2: Write the Essay

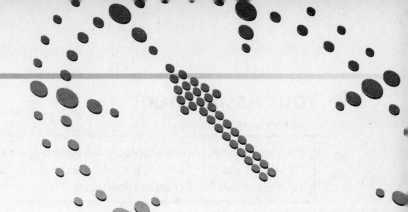

How much time do you have? Pay attention to the clock.

Plan and Write an Informative Essay

85 minutes

You will have 85 minutes to plan, write, revise, and edit your essay.

Your Plan

Before you start writing, think about the main idea of your essay. What is the most important point you want to make?

_____

_____

How do you plan to use the 85 minutes?

Estimated time for planning the essay?		minutes
Estimated time for writing?		minutes
Estimated time for editing?		minutes
Estimated time for checking spelling, grammar, and punctuation?		minutes
Total	**85**	**minutes**

Be sure to leave enough time for this step.

Notes:

_____

_____

_____

_____

Reread your essay, making sure that the points are clear. Check that there are no spelling or punctuation mistakes.

▶ Your Assignment

> You are preparing to write an informative essay on geocaching for health class. In researching the topic, you have identified two sources you will use in planning your essay.

After you have reviewed the sources, you must answer some questions about them. Briefly skim the sources and questions that follow. Then, go back and read the sources carefully so you will have the information you will need to answer the questions. Take notes on the sources as you read. You may refer back to your notes at any time during Part 1 or Part 2 of the performance task.

▶ Part 1 (35 minutes)

You will now read the sources. After carefully reading the sources, use the rest of the time in Part 1 to answer the three questions about them. Though your answers to these questions will help you think about what you have read and plan your essay, they will also be scored as part of the test.

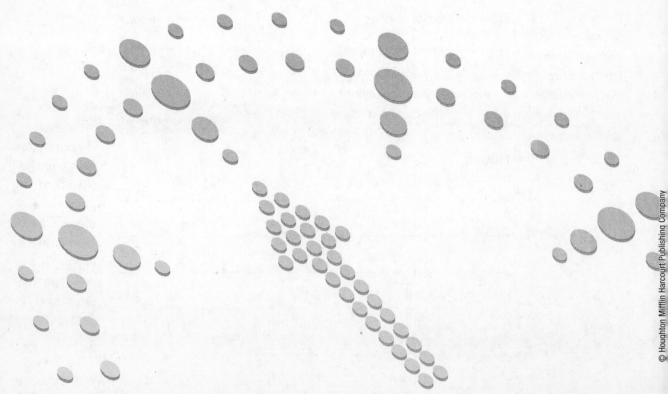

SOURCE #1:
Geocaching

by Amanda Briney,
Geography Guide for *About.com*   *August 2, 2009*

Geocaching is a worldwide outdoor hide-and-seek activity where participants use global positioning system (GPS) technology and latitude and longitude coordinates to locate containers, called geocaches or caches, that can be hidden anywhere in the world—from remote cliffs to along major highways. There are currently over 860,000 active geocaches located in over 100 countries on all continents, including Antarctica.

The word geocaching itself is derived from the use of "geo" for geography and "caching" as the process of hiding a cache. Cache is
10 a term used in computer technology terms to mean the storage of information in a computer's memory, but in hiking and camping the same term is applied to a hiding place for supplies. Thus when combined, geocaching means the use of geography, in this case GPS and maps, to find hidden containers.

History of Geocaching

Although similar to the older sports of letterboxing and orienteering in that it requires participants to navigate through unfamiliar terrain, geocaching is a relatively new activity. This is because it uses GPS and satellites to navigate and prior to the year 2000, GPS receivers were not accurate enough to allow users to find small
20 objects with a set of geographic coordinates. Before that year, selective availability, or the intentional disruption of satellite signals to GPS units causing errors of up to 328 feet (100 m), was in place for United States security purposes. On May 1, 2000 though, selective availability was turned off and almost immediately, the accuracy of personal GPS receivers increased.

With the removal of selective availability and increased accuracy with GPS, small objects could be more easily located with a set of geographic coordinates. On May 3, 2000, Dave Ulmer, a computer consultant from Oregon, hid a navigational target (a black bucket
30 containing various prizes and a logbook) in the woods to test the new GPS accuracy. He posted the coordinates of his target which were, N 45° 17.460 and W 122°24.800, online and within three days, two different users found the target.

The first person to find Ulmer's target was Mike Teague of Vancouver, Washington. Upon finding this target, he began looking up other newly placed targets around the world documenting them on his website. He then created a mailing list called "GPS Stash Hunt" to inform other users of new targets and the activity quickly grew in popularity.

40   Shortly thereafter, interested users began discussing different names for the activity because they believed "stash" could have a negative connotation and on May 30, 2000, Matt Stum suggested the name geocaching. "Geo," he said could be used to describe the geographic and global nature of the activity, while cache's meaning as a hiding place for items could be applied to the hiding of a target. In September 2000, geocaching became the official name for the activity and since then participation has grown worldwide.

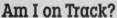

Am I on Track?

Actual Time Spent Reading

SOURCE #2:

Seattle Firm's GPS Scavenger-Hunt Game Stirs Controversy

by James Gunsalus, *Bloomberg News*   *November 14, 2006*

NOTES

Aaron McCain and his 9-year-old son rifled through a battered box containing rubber balls, napkin holders and plastic army men high on a pass near Mount Baker.

Using a handheld Global Positioning System device, the two had hiked miles to Excelsior Pass to find the hidden loot as part of a global scavenger hunt run by Seattle-based Geocaching.com. Players post coordinates on the Web site telling where they have hidden objects and challenge others to find the "caches" using GPS devices.

The adventure game, called "geocaching," started six years ago in
10 the Pacific Northwest and now counts more than 328,000 caches in 222 countries, the Web site says. The activity pushes people outdoors, although some parkland managers say they worry about its impact on sites ranging from sensitive forestlands to historic cemeteries.

Geocaching.com is the brainchild of Jeremy Irish, 33, a computer-software programmer who went on GPS scavenger hunts as a hobby. He quit his job at Savishopper.com, an online clothing store, to start the Web site in 2000.

His company, Groundspeak, employs 12 and has 500,000 registered users. He charges $30 a year for membership access to detailed,
20 interactive maps that help gamers navigate rough terrain and rivers.

The closely held company is profitable, though Irish said he isn't getting rich.

"I'm still living a meager lifestyle," he said. "We put the money back into the company."

GPS devices only recently have gone mainstream. The satellite navigation system was developed by the U.S. Defense Department, with the first launch in 1978. The U.S. Air Force disrupted signals for civilian users until 2000.

U.S. sales of the GPS units were $42.3 million last year, compared
30 with $16.7 million in 2002, according to the Boulder, Colo.-based Outdoor Industry Association's Web site.

Geocaching has stirred some controversy, however.

"If it's done right, it's actually a pretty good tool to introduce people to hiking and learning navigational skills," said the U.S. Forest Service's Gary Walker, lead climbing ranger on Mount St. Helens. "But I've also seen caches put on private property and people tromping all around looking for them."

The 242,000-acre Three Sisters Wilderness Area in Oregon banned geocaching in 2002. South Carolina has proposed fining people $100 for
40 placing caches without permission in cemeteries or at historic sites.

"Land managers get nervous about people wandering around in wilderness and want to keep them on trails," said Robert Speik, 78, a Bend, Ore., climbing instructor who fought a proposed ban in the nearby Badlands forest. "They lose sight of the fact that wilderness is where you wander."

McCain, a 32-year-old engineer who lives in Bellingham, said his family is responsible when hunting for caches.

"Finding the actual cache was pretty low on the list of exciting things that day," McCain said of his recent Excelsior Pass trip. "I got a
50 six-mile hike with my son, I saw the first colors of the fall and a peek at Mount Baker."

But geocaching bothers those who say satellites and computer screens interfere with the outdoors experience. The race to find caches sacrifices the slower pace needed to appreciate nature, said Scott Silver, director of Wild Wilderness, a nonprofit group in Bend.

Custodians for public lands in the Pacific Northwest wrestle with how to accommodate both sides.

The U.S. Bureau of Land Management proposed closing the 32,000-acre Badlands to geocachers in 2003, then yielded after enthusiasts
60 complained. Recreation manager Greg Currie says the bureau may revisit the issue.

"It places a big demand on the land managers to police these things, and we don't have staff or time for it."

Irish's Web site encourages geocachers to "Cache In, Trash Out"—that is, collect litter on trails. Manuals that come with some GPS devices include such tips as respecting private property and staying on trails.

Irish said he isn't worried about outdoor purists curbing the game's growth. Every January he doubles his computer-storage capacity as people receive that new handheld Christmas present.

70   "The idea of being a tech geek outside seemed like a good idea to me," he said. "I don't think I'm alone there."

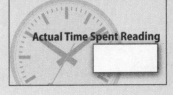

Am I on Track?

Actual Time Spent Reading

Part 1 Questions

Answer the following questions. Your answers to these questions will be scored. You may refer to your reading notes, and you should cite text evidence in your responses. You will be able to refer to your answers as you write your essay in Part 2.

1 **Prose Constructed-Response** Explain what geocaching is and what is required for the activity. Support your response with evidence from both sources.

_____

_____

_____

_____

_____

_____

2 Which of the following statements explains why geocaching is controversial?

   a. The word *cache* has a negative connotation.

   b. Geocachers have a tendency to take nature for granted.

   c. Outdoor purists are curbing the game's growth.

   d. Some people are disrespectful when they hide or hunt for caches.

3 Which piece of evidence best supports your answer to Question 2?

   a. "Shortly thereafter, interested users began discussing different names for the activity . . ." (Source #1, lines 42–43)

   b. "Manuals that come with some GPS devices include such tips as respecting private property and staying on trails." (Source #2, lines 65–66)

   c. "Every January he doubles his computer-storage capacity as people receive that new handheld Christmas present." (Source #2, lines 68–69)

   d. "Dave Ulmer, a computer consultant from Oregon, hid a navigational target . . . in the woods to test the new GPS accuracy." (Source #1, lines 30–33)

▶ Part 2 (85 minutes)

You will have 85 minutes to review your notes and sources, plan, draft, edit, and revise your essay. While you may use your notes and refer to the sources, your essay must represent your original work. You may refer to your responses to Part 1, but you cannot change those answers. Now read your assignment and the information about how your writing will be scored; then begin your work.

Your Assignment

It is time to start writing your informative essay about outdoor recreation. Your essay should explain what geocaching is and the controversy that surrounds it. When writing your essay, find ways to use information from the two sources to support your thesis. Be sure to present your ideas in a logical order.

Informative Essay Scoring

Your essay will be scored using the following:

1. **Organization/purpose:** How well did you state your thesis and support your thesis with a logical progression of ideas? Did you use a variety of transitions between ideas? Was your focus narrow enough to lead to a well-formed conclusion?

2. **Evidence/elaboration:** How well did you incorporate relevant information from the sources? How well did you elaborate your ideas? Did you use precise language appropriate to your audience and purpose?

3. **Conventions:** How well did you follow the rules of grammar, punctuation, capitalization, and spelling?

Now begin work on your essay. Manage your time carefully so that you can:

- plan your essay, using your notes
- write your essay
- revise and edit your final draft

© Houghton Mifflin Harcourt Publishing Company

Literary Analysis

Your language arts teacher has assigned your class a literary analysis of a poem by Robert Frost. You will need to use a biographical approach in analyzing the poem.

First you will review two sources that will help you with the biographical approach. The third source is Frost's poem. After you have reviewed these sources, you will answer some questions about them. You should first skim the sources and the questions and then go back and read them carefully.

In Part 2, you will write a literary analysis in which you analyze the poem "Out, Out—" using a biographical approach.

Time Management: Literary Analysis Task

Most formal writing tests are made up of two parts. Both parts of the tests are timed, so it's important to use your limited time wisely.

Part 1: Read Sources and Answer Questions

Preview the Assignment

35 minutes

You will have 35 minutes to read three sources. You will also answer questions about the sources .

How Many?

How many pages of reading?

How many multiple-choice questions?

How many prose constructed-response questions?

How do you plan to use the 35 minutes?

Estimated time to read:

Source #1: "Taking a Biographical Approach to Literary Criticism" .... minutes

Source #2: "A Biography: Robert Frost" .... minutes

Source #3: "Out, Out—" .... minutes

Estimated time to answer questions? .... minutes

Total   **35**   **minutes**

Any concerns?

_____

_____

_____

_____

Preview the questions so you'll know which information you'll need to find as you read.

35 minutes! That's not much time.

This is a lot to do in a short time.

Underline, circle, and take notes as you read. You probably won't have time to reread.

Part 2: Write the Analysis

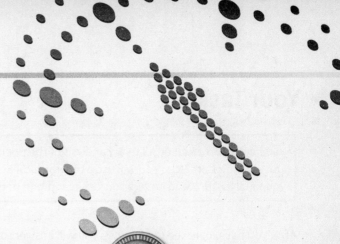

How much time do you have? Pay attention to the clock.

Plan and Write a Literary Analysis

85 minutes

You will have 85 minutes to plan, write, and edit your essay.

Your Plan

Before you start writing, decide how you will organize your literary analysis.

How do you plan to use the 85 minutes?

Estimated time for planning the essay?		minutes
Estimated time for writing?		minutes
Estimated time for editing?		minutes
Estimated time for checking spelling, grammar, and punctuation?		minutes
Total	**85**	**minutes**

Be sure to leave enough time for this step.

Notes:

_____

_____

_____

_____

_____

_____

Reread your essay, making sure that the points are clear. Check that there are no spelling or punctuation mistakes.

© Houghton Mifflin Harcourt Publishing Company

▶ Your Task

> You have been assigned a literary analysis of the poem "Out, Out—" by Robert Frost. You will use a biographical approach in your analysis, drawing on two sources in addition to the poem.

After you have reviewed the sources, you will answer some questions about them. Briefly skim the sources and the questions that follow. Then, go back and read the sources carefully so you will have the information you will need to answer the questions. Take notes on the sources as you read. You may refer back to your notes at any time during Part 1 or Part 2 of the performance task.

▶ Part 1 (35 minutes)

You will now read the sources. After carefully reading the sources, use the rest of the time in Part 1 to answer the five questions about them. Though your answers to these questions will help you think about what you have read and plan your essay, they will also be scored as part of the test.

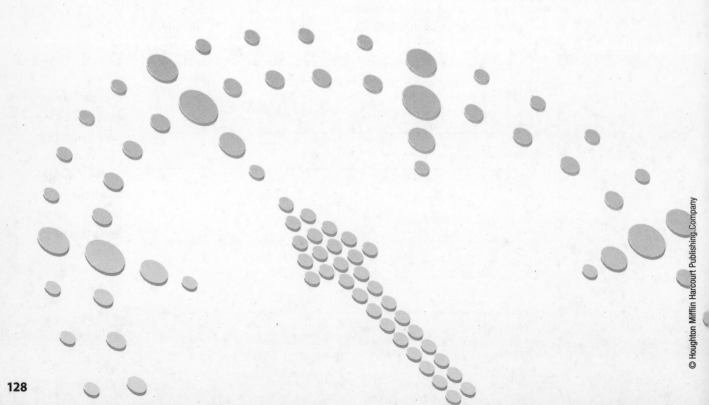

SOURCE #1:
Taking a Biographical Approach to Literary Criticism

by Kylene Beers

Read this conversation that I once had with a group of high school students. See if you've ever had a reaction like Adam's.

"So, what do you think about the story?" I asked.

"I liked it," some said. Others just nodded. Some just sat.

"Well, what can you tell me about the author from reading this story?" I asked.

Silence for a while and finally Adam said, "I didn't read anything about the author. I just read the story."

Adam was right—he did just read the story—but he was also wrong.
10 When reading a story or a poem, you can sometimes make inferences, or guesses, about its writer. Consider this situation: You read a story about a character who suffers through a tough experience, but in the end is celebrated for her bravery. You can guess that the author believes that bravery should be rewarded.

You can't always presume, however, that a writer has had the same experiences that he or she writes about. For example, you can't presume that a writer lived through the events he or she describes in a short story about a high school athlete, even though the writer might have been a high school athlete herself. You can conclude, however, that the writer
20 understands what it is *like* to compete in high school athletics.

Sometimes, however, a writer does use a personal experience or an actual event in a short story or poem. Frost's poem "Out, Out—" is based on a real-life incident recorded in the *Littleton Courier*, a New Hampshire newspaper, on March 31, 1901, in which a boy suffers a serious accident to his hand. Frost's treatment of the subject takes into account not only the tragic story of this accident, but also Frost's own experiences. Your job as a critic is to evaluate how the author's life is evident in what he or she wrote.

30 Clearly, authors bring their education, experiences, and interests with them to the page. A biographical approach to literary criticism means that you think about an author's life experiences as you respond to and analyze a text as a reader.

You can practice using a biographical approach to literary criticism by reading the following biography of Robert Frost and by applying what you learn about him as you respond to his poem "Out, Out—."

Am I on Track?

Actual Time Spent Reading

SOURCE #2:
A Biography: Robert Frost

by Julio Silvera

Winner of four Pulitzer Prizes for poetry, Robert Frost (1874–1963) was for years the best-known poet in the United States. Although Frost was born in San Francisco, he was raised in New England, which became the setting for nearly all his poetry. As a young man, Frost had tried raising chickens on a farm that his grandfather had given him, but he was unsuccessful. He also had a difficult time selling his poems. In 1912, after the deaths of two of his children, he and his family moved to England. There, Frost met with success. He found a publisher for his first two collections of poems (*A Boy's Will* and *North of Boston*). The

10   books were popular immediately, and by the time Frost returned to the United States, publishers were interested in his work.

Frost lived in New England for most of his life and was known as the New England poet. He found his subjects in the landscapes and people of New England, especially in New Hampshire and Vermont. In his poems he deliberately used the everyday language he heard in conversations with farmers. The plain speech and simple, everyday subjects of his poems disguise their complex thoughts. Frost once wrote that a subject for poetry ". . . should be common in experience and uncommon in books. . . . It should have happened to everyone but it

20   should have occurred to no one before as material."

Frost spent the rest of his long life farming, writing poetry, giving lectures, and reading his poems to audiences. As he put it, he liked to "say," rather than recite, his poetry. However, Frost never read his poem "Out, Out—" in public because he felt it was "too cruel." Like the title's allusion to a famous speech made by Shakespeare's Macbeth upon learning of his wife's death, the poem, too, is filled with bitterness about the brevity of life—of its being a "brief candle" that can be snuffed out in an instant.

Am I on Track?

Actual Time Spent Reading

SOURCE #3:
"Out, Out—"

by Robert Frost

NOTES

The buzz saw snarled and rattled in the yard
And made dust and dropped stove-length sticks of wood,
Sweet-scented stuff when the breeze drew across it.
And from there those that lifted eyes could count
5   Five mountain ranges one behind the other
Under the sunset far into Vermont.
And the saw snarled and rattled, snarled and rattled,
As it ran light, or had to bear a load.
And nothing happened: day was all but done.
10 Call it a day, I wish they might have said
To please the boy by giving him the half hour
That a boy counts so much when saved from work.
His sister stood beside them in her apron
To tell them "Supper." At the word, the saw,
15 As if to prove saws knew what supper meant,
Leaped out at the boy's hand, or seemed to leap—
He must have given the hand. However it was,
Neither refused the meeting. But the hand!
The boy's first outcry was a rueful laugh,
20 As he swung toward them holding up the hand,
Half in appeal, but half as if to keep
The life from spilling. Then the boy saw all—
Since he was old enough to know, big boy
Doing a man's work, though a child at heart—
25 He saw all spoiled. "Don't let him cut my hand off—
The doctor, when he comes. Don't let him, sister!"
So. But the hand was gone already.
The doctor put him in the dark of ether.
He lay and puffed his lips out with his breath.
30 And then—the watcher at his pulse took fright.
No one believed. They listened at his heart.
Little—less—nothing!—and that ended it.
No more to build on there. And they, since they
Were not the one dead, turned to their affairs.

Am I on Track?

Actual Time Spent Reading

Part 1 Questions

Answer the following questions. Your answers to these questions will be scored. You may refer to your reading notes, and you should cite text evidence in your responses. You will be able to refer to your answers as you write your essay in Part 2.

1 What does the word *rueful* mean in these lines from Source #3?

> "The boy's first outcry was a rueful laugh,
> As he swung toward them holding up the hand,
> Half in appeal, but half as if to keep
> The life from spilling. Then the boy saw all—
> Since he was old enough to know, big boy
> Doing a man's work, though a child at heart—"
> (lines 19–24)

- **a.** apologetic
- **b.** shocked
- **c.** hysterical
- **d.** grieving

2 Which phrase from the lines of text in Question 1 best helps you understand the meaning of *rueful*?

- **a.** "As he swung toward them"
- **b.** "holding up the hand"
- **c.** "Then the boy saw all"
- **d.** "though a child at heart"

3 Which of the following sentences provides an accurate statement one could make after reading the three sources?

- **a.** The title of the poem "Out, Out—" is an allusion to a famous speech in Shakespeare's play *Hamlet*.
- **b.** Frost thought that a poem should be based on a common experience that people had read about before in a work of fiction.
- **c.** Frost based his poem on an actual incident that was reported in a New Hampshire newspaper on March 31, 1901.
- **d.** A reader's response to a literary text always takes an author's life experiences into account.

4 Select **three** pieces of evidence from the three sources that support your answer to Question 3.

   a. "You can't always presume, however, that a writer has had the same experiences that he or she writes about." (Source #1, lines 15–16)

   b. "Sometimes, however, a writer does use a personal experience or an actual event in a short story or poem." (Source #1, lines 21–22)

   c. ". . . based on a real-life incident recorded in . . . a New Hampshire newspaper, on March 31, 1901 . . ." (Source #1, lines 23–24)

   d. "Clearly, authors bring their education, experiences, and interests with them to the page." (Source #1, lines 29–30)

   e. "He found his subjects in the landscapes and people of New England, especially in New Hampshire and Vermont."(Source #2, lines 13–14)

   f. "Frost spent the rest of his long life farming, writing poetry, giving lectures, and reading his poems to audiences." (Source #2, lines 21–22)

   g. "However, Frost never read his poem 'Out, Out—' in public because he felt it was 'too cruel.'" (Source #2, lines 23–24)

   h. " . . . And they, since they / Were not the one dead, turned to their affairs." (Source #3, lines 33–34)

5 Prose Constructed-Response Based on the information found in the three sources, write a paragraph that explains how taking a biographical approach to literary criticism can help you make inferences about a writer's life and how these inferences can help you interpret the text. Cite textual evidence to support your ideas.

_____

_____

_____

_____

_____

_____

_____

_____

_____

_____

_____

_____

_____

_____

_____

_____

_____

_____

▶ Part 2 (85 minutes)

You will have 85 minutes to review your notes and sources, plan, draft, edit, and revise your essay. While you may use your notes and refer to the sources, your essay must represent your original work. You may refer to your responses to Part 1, but you cannot change those answers. Now read your assignment and the information about how your writing will be scored; then begin your work.

Your Assignment

It is time to begin your literary analysis. Think about Frost's poem, using what you have learned from the two other sources. Make sure that you include quotations from all three sources and that you present your ideas in a logical order.

Literary Analysis Scoring

Your literary analysis will be scored using the following:

1. **Organization/purpose:** How well did you state your thesis/controlling idea and support it with a logical progression of ideas? Did you use a variety of transitions between ideas? Was your controlling idea narrow enough to lead to a logical conclusion?

2. **Evidence/elaboration:** How well did you incorporate relevant information from the sources? How well did you elaborate your ideas? Did you use precise language appropriate to your audience and purpose?

3. **Conventions:** How well did you follow the rules of grammar, punctuation, capitalization, and spelling?

Now begin work on your essay. Manage your time carefully so that you can:

- plan your essay, using your notes

- write your essay

- revise and edit your final draft

Acknowledgments

"10 Great Things Teens Learn While 'Playing' Online" from *About.com,* www.familyinternet.about.com. Text copyright © 2013 by Christie Matte. Reprinted by permission of About, Inc.

"700 Lire Presenting the Edict Single" (Retitled: "How 1582 Lost Ten Days") from *Smithsonian Institution,* www.arago.si.edu. Text copyright © 2002-2013 by Smithsonian Institution. Reprinted by permission of Smithsonian Institution.

"Camouflaging the Chimera" from *Pleasure Dome: New and Selected Poems* by Yusef Komunyakaa. Text copyright © 1993 by Yusef Komunyakaa. Reprinted by permission of Wesleyan University Press.

"Geocaching" by Amanda Briney from *About.com,* http://geography. about.com. Text copyright © 2013 by Amanda Briney. Reprinted by permission of About, Inc.

"Out, Out-" from *The Poetry of Robert Frost* by Robert Frost, edited by Edward Connery Lathem. Text copyright © 1916, 1969 by Henry Holt and Company. Text copyright © 1944 by Robert Frost. Reprinted by permission of Henry Holt and Company, LLC.

Excerpt from "Pro/Con: Should Student Service Learning Hours Be Mandatory for High School Graduation?" by Claire Koenig & Simrin Gupta from *Silver Chips Online,* March 10, 2011, www.silverchips.mbhs. edu. Text copyright © 2011 by Silver Chips. Reprinted by permission of Silver Chips.

"Seattle Firm's GPS Scavenger-Hunt Game Stirs Controversy" by James Gunsalus from *The Seattle Times.* Text copyright © 2009 by James Gunsalus. Reprinted by permission of The Seattle Times Company.

"Sonnet XXX of Fatal Interview" from *Collected Poems* by Edna St. Vincent Millay. Text copyright © 1931, 1958 by Edna St. Vincent Millay and Norma Millay Ellis. All rights reserved. Reprinted by permission of Holly Peppe, Literary Executor, The Millay Society.

"Teens and the Internet: How Much Is Too Much?" by Stephanie Newman, Ph.D. from *Psychology Today,* April 6, 2010. Text copyright © 2010 by Psychology Today. Reprinted by permission of Sussex Publishers, LLC.